(PAGE 1) *Rumpelstiltskin's carriage interior lighting key* • *Mike Hernandez* – digital
(ABOVE) *Alcove detail* • Design – *Paul Westacott*, Color – *Griselda Sastrawinata* – digital
(RIGHT) *Rumpelstiltskin's throne room concept sketch* • *Paul Westacott* – pencil

INSIGHT EDITIONS

3160 Kerner Blvd., Suite 108
San Rafael, CA 94901

www.insighteditions.com

Library of Congress Cataloging-
in-Publication Data available.

ISBN: 978-1-60887-002-8

10 9 8 7 6 5 4 3 2 1

Manufactured in China by
Palace Press International
www.palacepress.com

ROOTS of PEACE   REPLANTED PAPER

Palace Press International, in association
with Roots of Peace, will plant two trees for
each tree used in the manufacturing of this
book. Roots of Peace is an internationally
renowned humanitarian organization
dedicated to eradicating land mines
worldwide and converting war-torn lands
into productive farms and wildlife habitats.
Together, we will plant two million fruit and
nut trees in Afghanistan and provide farmers
there with the skills and support necessary
for sustainable land use.

Other INSIGHT EDITIONS
animation books include:
Shrek: The Art of the Quest
The Art of Kung Fu Panda
The Art of Madagascar: Escape 2 Africa
The Art and Making of
Cloudy with a Chance of Meatballs
The Art of Planet 51
Surf's Up: The Art and Making of a True Story
The Art of Open Season
The Art and Making of Monster House

The Art of
DreamWorks
Shrek
Forever After

Foreword by Cameron Diaz

Written by Jerry Schmitz

INSIGHT EDITIONS

San Rafael, California

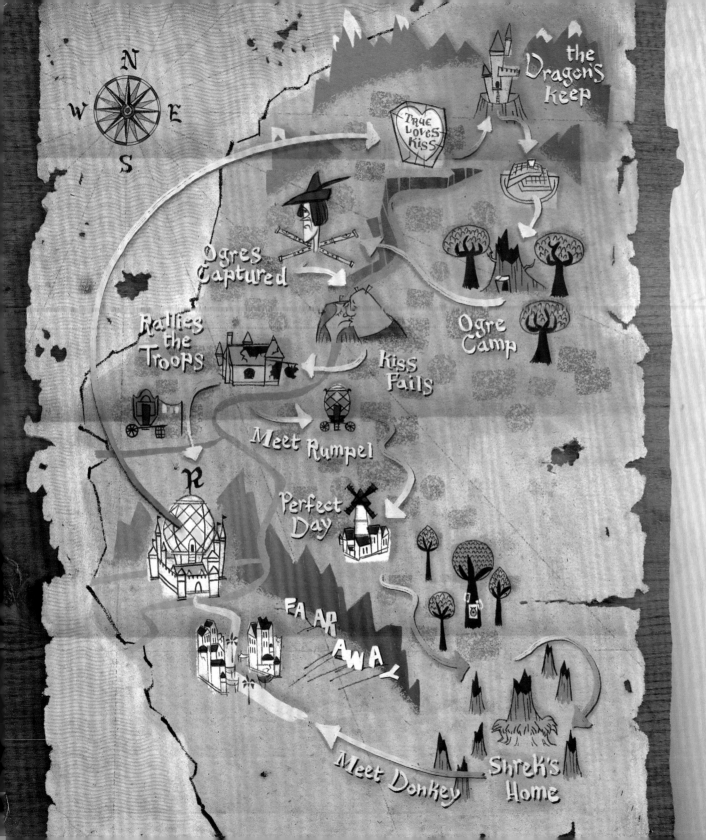

the Dragon's keep

TRUE LOVES KISS

Ogres Captured

Rallies the Troops

Kiss Fails

Ogre Camp

Meet Rumpel

R

Perfect Day

FA AR AWAY

Meet Donkey

Shrek's Home

WANTED

OGRES

REWARD

WANTED

OGRES

REWARD

WANTED

OGRES

REWARD

(FAR LEFT) *Sequence map* • *Leighton Hickman* – digital
(LEFT) *Ogres wanted posters* • *Ron Kurniawan* – digital
(TOP) *Table top map* • *Leighton Hickman* – digital
(ABOVE) *Path to Far Far Away map* • *Peter Zaslav* – digital

Contents

Foreword

I REMEMBER WHEN I GOT THE CALL about lending my voice to the first Shrek adventure. I had never worked on an animated film, but it sounded like a lot of fun.

When I showed up at the studio to begin recording Fiona's voice for the first time, I knew very little about the long, complicated process of creating an animated film. Now, four movies later, I can proudly say that I know the difference between a rigger and a layout artist, and I am simply in awe of the visual development and character design artists. In fact, I've come to think that making an animated movie is like building a house—the story serves as the foundation, the actors are the framework, and the various animation departments provide the wiring, walls, paint, and roof. It's been so great to work with these talented artists, animators, and filmmakers who never cease to amaze me with their brilliant ability to bring these characters and stories to life.

Most of all, I am so proud to have provided the voice for Princess Fiona. She is not only an amazing character, but a terrific role model. It's been wonderful to be part of her evolution from a pampered princess who believes in only one type of happy ending to a content ogre/wife/mother, as well as a tough warrior princess in the latest movie! It is so gratifying to me when kids (and their parents) see me and say, "Do you know who that is? That's Princess Fiona." I never get tired of hearing that! It also brings me great joy to be able to share a project of mine with my nieces and nephew.

Whichever character you best relate to, or whoever makes you laugh the most, the pages of this book are a testament to the incredible talents of the crew that made *Shrek Forever After*—as well as the artists who worked on all the other Shrek films. It's been great fun playing in this world, and for that I extend a heartfelt thank you to the filmmakers and everyone at DreamWorks Animation.

—*Cameron Diaz*

(RIGHT) ***Fiona revealed*** • *Peter Zaslav* – digital

Introduction

BY NOW, THE FRACTURED FAIRYTALE OF SHREK AND FIONA and their adventures in the magical land of Far Far Away is well known. Based on the popular children's book *Shrek!* by William Steig, the films have received critical praise, worldwide box-office success, and the first-ever Academy Award® for Best Animated Feature. Suffice it to say, Shrek and the characters of Far Far Away have earned their rightful place in cinema and animation history.

With three successful movies to the franchise's credit, and a lot of fairytale territory already covered, the filmmakers at DreamWorks Animation were faced with an exciting challenge when they embarked on the final chapter in the adventures of Shrek and Fiona. Always envisioned as a multi-part story, the specifics of Shrek's last outing were still to be finalized. Director Mike Mitchell, a veteran of two previous Shrek films, set the challenge: "How do we make the same thing that everyone has seen, give the audience what they want, but in a way that's even more beautiful than anyone would ever expect?" In other words, how do you craft an emotional story that engages the audience and yet

concludes the story of Shrek and Fiona in a fresh and satisfying way?

Joining Mitchell on the production were accomplished producers Teresa Cheng and Gina Shay, both of whom brought an enormous amount of animation experience to the film. Cheng was co-producer on *Madagascar* and had most recently served as producer on the popular holiday special *Shrek the Halls*. Shay's credits include *The SpongeBob SquarePants Movie*, among many others. "Mike, Gina, and Teresa are a great team," praises executive producer Aron Warner, who has produced all the Shrek movies. "They create a worry-free situation for me!"

Together, Mitchell, Cheng, and Shay assembled a crew of visual development and storyboard artists, character animators, modeling, rigging, and lighting teams, layout artists, and visual effects technicians. Their choices brought together a number of creative minds new to the world of Shrek with a host of others who had worked on the prior three films and were excited to conclude this story in 3D—a first for Shrek. "There's a lot of love on this crew," declares Shay. "We're all self-professed fans of Shrek and everyone brought so much of that passion to

the table, which resulted in a really amazing, collaborative environment."

And when Shay says "fans of Shrek," she means fans of none other than the big green guy himself. This love for the eponymous hero meant that when it came time to develop the story for *Shrek Forever After,* the filmmakers kept their attentions and the focus of the film on Shrek himself.

Shrek has become somewhat domesticated after three films. Now the father of three, he has responsibilities, duties, and obligations. He is no longer the intimidating ogre we met at the beginning of the first film who caused the people of Far Far Away to run screaming in the other direction. Now they ask him to sign their pitchforks!

As with most continuing stories, every journey and chapter brings new experiences and opportunities for a character to grow and develop. In the case of Shrek, given his predicament, the next logical step seemed to be a midlife crisis of sorts. "We knew we had to keep the story fresh, and give it a new twist," explains Cheng. "We asked ourselves, 'What more can Shrek learn on his journey as an ogre?'"

Early in the development process, artists came up with an image of Shrek looking at himself in the mirror and staring at his old "Wanted" poster while thinking to himself, "What have I become?" For the filmmakers, this image proved to be a significant turning point in the development of the story. "We thought it was interesting that he's not the ogre he was in the first *Shrek.* He's domesticated; he's not scary—he's beloved," says Mitchell. "And quite honestly," the director adds, "the last thing we wanted was for Shrek to lose his edge."

At that point, writer Josh Klausner came up with the concept of Shrek having to win Fiona's love all over again in an alternate universe by going back in time. "That turned into a very relatable wish fulfillment," says Mitchell. "We all think of returning to our past, turning the clock back to live life over."

With these core themes of self-examination and time travel in mind, the filmmakers began to weave a tale wherein Shrek begins to wonder who he's become and what life might have been like if he were still a

(Opposite) *Shrek and Fiona fight concept* • *Felix Yoon* – digital
(Right) *Rumpelstiltskin concept sketch* • *Max Boas* – pencil

lone ogre in the swamp. "That seemed like a great place to start," adds Shay. "Shrek starts to ask himself a lot of questions. 'Who is Shrek?' We really wanted to go back to the basics and the root of his journey. We knew this film really needed to be Shrek's story, told through his eyes."

For Walt Dohrn, who served as head of story on *Shrek Forever After*, the premise fit nicely into the world of Shrek. "In the first film, Shrek learns to love himself; in the second, he learns what it is like to be part of a family; in *Shrek the Third*, he comes to terms with accepting the responsibility of being a father and husband. In the fourth and final film, he learns about the bigger picture of being loved by the world and, more importantly, being part of a loving and supportive community."

For Mitchell, relating to the story and Shrek's feelings was easy. The father of two toddlers, he could empathize with "Shrek the dad," who has to forego the traditional life of a rough-and-tumble ogre for that of a Saturday afternoon soccer shuttle driver. "I have a two-year-old and a four-year-old," explains Mitchell. "When I took this job, my second child was born. It really is a life-changing experience, and it is very hard to be cool when you have a diaper bag strapped across your shoulder and a pacifier around your neck."

With that direction in mind, the crew developed a classic "What if . . . ?" story for Shrek. Now happily married with three kids, Shrek's life has become mundane and very routine (at least in his eyes). Feeling somewhat nostalgic for his ogre bachelor days, Shrek makes a deal with the proverbial devil, who in this particular case is none other than the classic fairytale schemer Rumpelstiltskin.

The newest villain to the world of Shrek, Rumpelstiltskin is after one thing: the Kingdom of Far Far Away. Capitalizing on Shrek's longing for the old days, Rumpel makes Shrek an offer he can't refuse: to live a day free of responsibility, as a *real* ogre. In exchange, all Shrek has to do is give Rumpel one day from his past. Seems like a fair trade—a day for a day. Little does Shrek know that the day Rumpel decides to take will change history rather dramatically both for Shrek and the inhabitants of Far Far Away. In an elegant gesture of calculated evil, Rumpel chooses

(Right) ***Palace paintings*** • *Felix Yoon* – digital
(Opposite) ***Far Far Away concept*** • *Griselda Sastrawinata* – digital

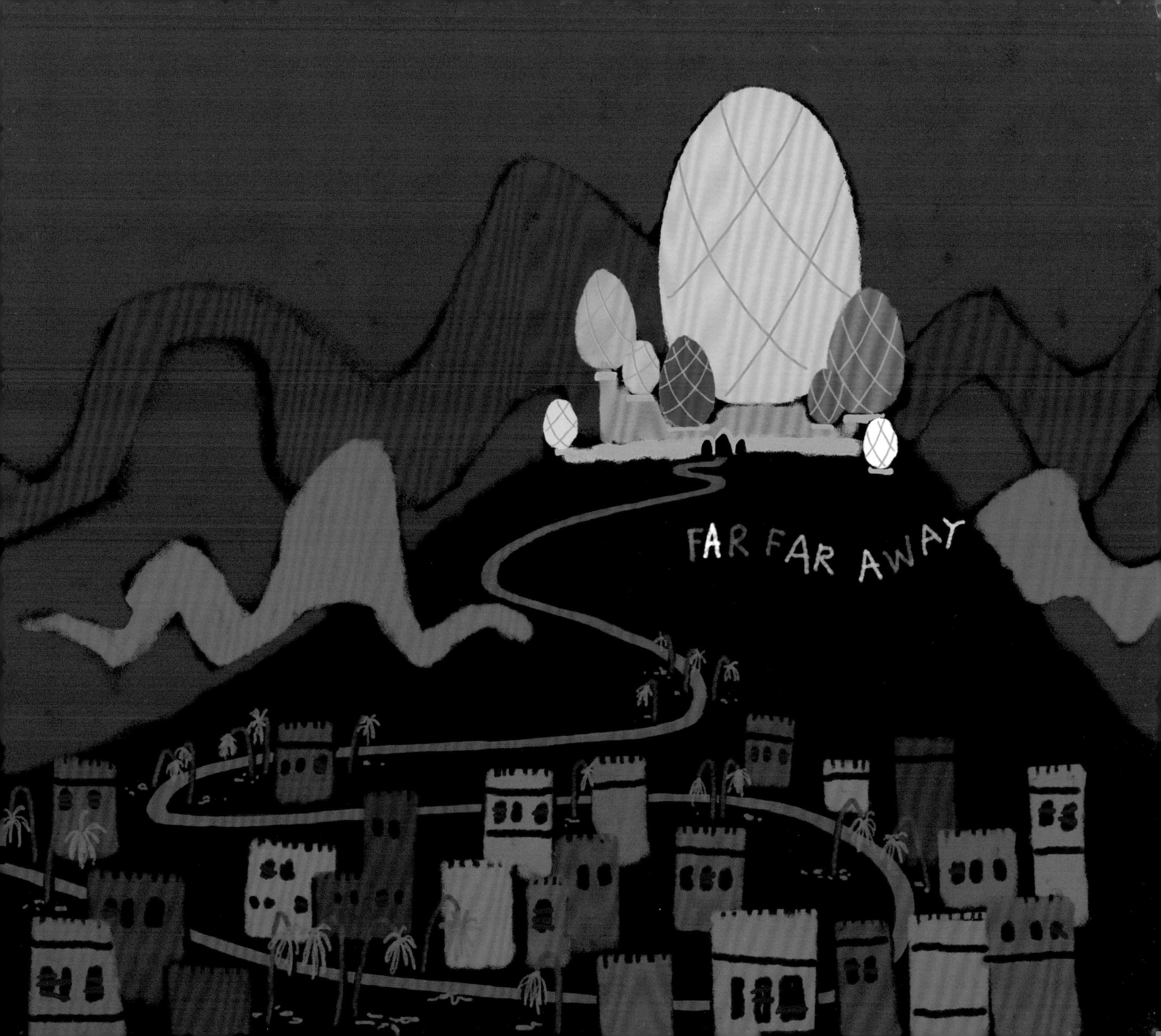
FAR FAR AWAY

"We embraced 3D as a storytelling device from the first frame of the movie. Our goal was to immerse our audience in Shrek's world so they see the story unfold from Shrek's point of view. Cinematography, design, and lighting have to work in tandem to draw the audience fully into the story."

—*Teresa Cheng*, producer

none other than the day Shrek was born. "The result is nothing short of catastrophic," says Mitchell. "Everything the audience knows about Shrek, Fiona, and the fairytale characters is turned upside down and thrown into an alternate reality."

One might think that introducing an "alternate reality" would give the crew carte blanche when it came to the look and design of the film, almost as if they could start from scratch, but that was not entirely the case. "It was a real challenge when we set out to define the look of the film," says Mitchell. "We really wanted to give this film a different look but at the same time be true to the world of Shrek."

Mitchell, Cheng, and Shay were inspired by the look that production designer Peter Zaslav had created for the holiday special *Shrek the Halls*, which he worked on with Cheng and Shay. *Shrek the Halls* "was the first time I had seen Shrek and Fiona's house covered in snow," explains Mitchell. "It was familiar, it was the same, but it wasn't. I knew then that we would be able to pull off the alternate reality from a design perspective."

Zaslav was brought on board, along with art director Max Boas. To

create a visual template, Zaslav and Boas started with the familiar shape language and color palette established in the first three films. "Basically, the film starts out as a visual continuation of the previous Shrek films," explains Zaslav.

The artists even amped up the colors just a notch in order to highlight the dramatic contrast when Shrek finds himself in the alternate reality. "It's even brighter, happier, and more colorful than *Shrek 2* and *Shrek the Third*—that is, until Shrek signs his contract with Rumpelstiltskin and we catch a glimpse of Far Far Away ruled by Rumpel."

As soon as Shrek is stranded in the alternate reality of Far, Far Away, the look, tone, and color of the film shift dramatically. A once lush, verdant landscape, Far Far Away becomes a somewhat desolate, barren, and dark wasteland dominated by gold, greens, and greys— inspired in part by the colors of the contract Shrek signs with Rumpel, especially the gold ink.

(ABOVE) **Shrek at the mirror** • *Felix Yoon* – digital
(OPPOSITE) **Ogre warrior concepts** • *Patrick Mate* – digital
(RIGHT) **Rumpelstiltskin's ink bottle concept** • *Leighton Hickman* – digital

> **"To have a ticking clock built into your story is both a blessing and a curse."**
> —*Mike Mitchell*, director

Gold, as one would expect of a tale involving the fairytale character who once promised Rapunzel he could spin hay into 24-karat thread, became an important touchstone for designing the alternate reality ruled by the infamous Rumpel. "Gold has become a dominant visual theme associated with Rumpelstiltskin and that actually gets propagated to the entire environment," explains Zaslav. "We've gotten used to the world of Shrek—all the green trees, the lush green grass. In the alternate reality, all that green gives way to more yellows and golds."

But this gold does not glitter. It is instead the gold of harvest time—the gold of fall, when things begin to decay, which provides a rather stark contrast to the green of spring that typically animates the Shrek color scheme. This visual difference created a lot of creative opportunities for the filmmakers. "It's been a lot of fun turning the world upside down and playing up the contrast between Shrek's normal reality and watching him navigate his way through this surreal world with swirling clouds and barren trees," says Boas.

The darkness of the landscape reinforces, too, the initial bleakness of Shrek's predicament. Working these dark dimensions into the overall upbeat mood of the Shrek franchise was challenging. "The world is going to be a little darker, and a lot of this movie happens at night," explains Cheng. "One of our biggest challenges was to let the story unfold over 24 hours—to still have that 'ticking clock' feeling, but not live in darkness for too much of the film."

To contrast with the dark tones of the film, the filmmakers devised a

But ultimately, technology serves the story—so the filmmakers stayed committed to their vision of an emotionally compelling tale. "If we've done our jobs, you'll believe in this world," says Cheng. "You'll feel it rather than see it."

In approaching the more emotionally driven sequences in the script where the mental state of the characters needed to be clearly illustrated, Dohrn and Mitchell urged the story artists to begin by temporarily setting aside the more logistical "bells and whistles" production side of a giant CG 3D animated feature film to focus mainly on the minimal expressions of character. "Not minimal as in simple," explains Dohrn, "but minimal in the sense that there is a pure, heartfelt immediacy to the delicate hand-drawn line from the story artist that best represents the core of a character's feelings."

Even the most subtle shift of an eyebrow's position can make a character go from expressing frustration to conveying regret. "There was always subtext to the scene, especially with a character like Shrek, who has a hard time articulating his feelings," says Dohrn. "In a scene where he appears to be expressing a frustrated anger, we knew deep down he's struggling with issues of self-worth. This would help dictate a more engaging, layered performance, in our boards and ultimately in the final film."

In a fitting challenge for the final installment of the Shrek films, Shrek once again needs to save Far Far Away, win the heart of Fiona, and prove that he is worthy of True Love's Kiss. Only then can he save himself and return to his old, familiar world and life. In so doing, Shrek comes to terms with the life he briefly left behind, and by choosing it again becomes truly ready, willing, and able to live out his Happily Ever After. . . .

number of new locations, environments, and characters that would liven things up and create some new opportunities for humor in this changed world. This led to an absurdist and decadent approach to Rumpelstiltskin and his army of witches, as well as his opulent, over-the-top palace, Rumpeland, which is an elaborate visual feast.

This commitment to lavish, stunning imagery was furthered with a suite of innovative visual effects. The first of the Shrek films to be shot in 3D stereoscopic vision, *Shrek Forever After* was carefully planned as a fully realized 3D universe. Doug Cooper, who led the visual effects team, says, "3D is an equal partner in everything we do. We don't look at it as an afterthought. We've given a lot of careful thought to the staging of our shots—designing them to take advantage of stereo."

"The fact that we are doing this movie in 3D has complemented our attempt to expand the universe," says Zaslav. "We're literally building the sets out in all dimensions, something we've never done."

(ABOVE) *Candy Apple sign* • *Felix Yoon* – digital
(RIGHT) *Ogre doll* • *Leighton Hickman* – digital
(OPPOSITE) *Dragon's flight lighting key* • *Leighton Hickman* – digital

15

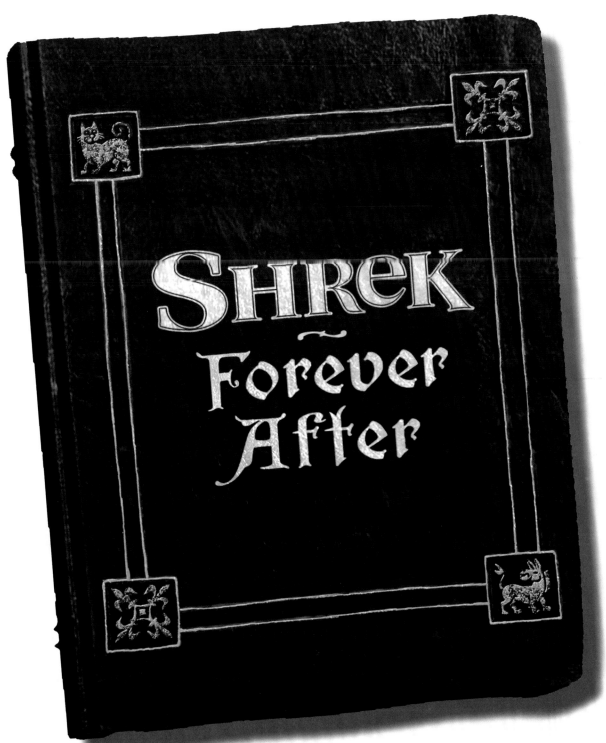

SHREK
~
Forever
After

(Left) *Storybook cover* • *Paul Duncan* – digital
(Above & Opposite) *Storybook sketches & pages* •
Griselda Sastrawinata – digital

*In the tradition of every Shrek film that has
come before,* Shrek Forever After *opens with
a storybook prologue. Griselda Sastrawinata
created the panels for* Shrek Forever After's
*opening sequence in her unique style. Narrated
by Rumpelstiltskin, the prologue reminds us of
Shrek and Fiona's early courtship. Through a
flashback to King Harold and Queen Lilian's
clandestine meeting with Rumpelstiltskin, and
the deal that was never signed thanks to Shrek
rescuing Fiona, we come to understand why
Rumpel angrily rips the last few pages out
of the book.*

 Once upon a time a long time ago FAR FAR AWAY — a KING and a QUEEN had a beautiful daughter named ✳ ✳ FIONA ✳ ✳

 But she was possessed by a TERRIBLE CURSE BY DAY, A LOVELY PRINCESS — BY NIGHT, A HIDEOUS OGRE

 Only TRUE LOVE'S KISS COULD LIFT HER CURSE — ✳✳✳ and so FIONA WAITED ✳✳✳ IN A TOWER GUARDED BY A DRAGON UNTIL THE DAY WHEN HER TRUE LOVE WOULD ARRIVE

 As the days ✳✳✳ TURNED INTO YEARS the KING and QUEEN — WERE FORCED ✳✳✳ TO RESORT TO MORE ✳✳✳ DESPERATE MEASURES

 No one ◆◆◆◆◆ WOULD HAVE GUESSED THAT AN OGRE NAMED SHREK ◆ — WHOSE ROAR WAS ✳✳ FEARED ✳✳ THROUGHOUT THE LAND

 WOULD SAVE THE ◆ BEAUTIFUL ◆ PRINCESS FIONA

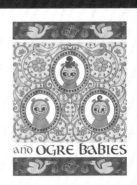 TRUE LOVE'S KISS LED TO MARRIAGE — and OGRE BABIES

 And the kingdom of FAR FAR AWAY was finally at peace FAR FAR AWAY — And they lived h·a·p·p·i·l·y

 ✳◆✳ EVER ✳◆✳ — AFTER

PART 1
Domestic Bliss

The Swamp House

To illustrate just how domesticated Shrek's life has become, the art department developed a number of props and set dressings to create the cluttered atmosphere you might expect to find in a busy household with three toddlers. No longer an ogre bachelor's pad, the tree stump has become overrun with Fergus, Farkle, and Felicia's toys, trinkets, and laundry. At left is an early sketch of Felicia's favorite doll, Sir Squeakles, who plays a key role in the movie.

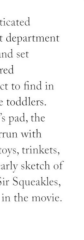

(Above) *Ogre doll sketch* • *Leighton Hickman* – digital
(Right) *Ogre baby toy designs* • *Paul Duncan* – digital
(Below) *Skrek's living room lighting key* • *Peter Zaslav* – digital

(Above) *Taking out the trash lighting keys* • *Paul Duncan* – digital

(Above) **Shrek's front yard concept** • *Peter Zaslav & Mike Hernandez* – digital

(Below) **Dinner at the swamp** • *Natalie Franscioni-Karp* – digital

Fairytale Characters

LIKE SHREK, the familiar fairytale characters that inhabit Far Far Away have settled into routine domestic lives at the beginning of *Shrek Forever After*. Shown here in early storyboard sequences, the Three Little Pigs, Pinocchio, and even the Big Bad Wolf now work at the Candy Apple (the establishment formerly known as the Poison Apple).

(ABOVE) **Candy Apple band storyboard** • *Justin Hunt* – digital

(ABOVE) **Dinner storyboard** • *Dave Smith* – digital

(ABOVE) **Birthday bash** • *Justin Hunt* – digital

(ABOVE) **Dragon flying over** • *Raman Hui* – digital

22

"We wanted the audience to be learning things as Shrek is learning them."

—*Mike Mitchell,* director

One early story draft included a flashback sequence of Shrek during his teen years. Design sketches by Patrick Mate shown here indicate that even ogres go through an awkward phase.

(LEFT & BELOW) *Teen Shrek character design sketches* • *Patrick Mate* – digital

Everyone has a breaking point. Shrek's comes in the form of an obnoxious young lad named Butterpants. Whiny, pampered, and spoiled by his dad, Butterpants harasses Shrek into roaring for him. Add a grating voice (supplied by director Mike Mitchell) and you've got a character who's more than enough to send any ogre over the edge.

(RIGHT) *Butterpants character sketch* • *Patrick Mate* – pencil

The Candy Apple

To celebrate the ogre triplets' first birthday, Shrek's neighborhood bar gets a complete makeover. Drawing inspiration from establishments where children are given free rein and parents are rendered helpless in a festive, sugarcoated atmosphere, the production team took the basic structure of the Poison Apple and transformed it into the Candy Apple. Bright pinks and blues replaced the original browns and yellows and somber shadows, and the pool table and dartboards were swapped out for medieval versions of arcade games and puppet shows. One remnant of the Poison Apple did manage to survive: Doris the barmaid finds a new calling as the Candy Apple's head waitress.

(Opposite) *Sir Duck's of Cheez-a-lot concept* • *Jon Klassen* – digital

(Above) *Unicorny's concept* • *Griselda Sastrawinata* – digital

(Above) *Game concepts* • *Griselda Sastrawinata* – digital
(Below) *Waitress Doris concept* • *Griselda Sastrawinata* – digital

(Above) *Mascot costume concepts* • *Griselda Sastrawinata* – digital

(Above) *Game concept* • *Paul Westacott* – digital
(Below) *Barrel labels* • *Paul Duncan* – digital

(Above) *Jam band* • *Griselda Sastrawinata* – digital
(Below) *Jam band* • *Paul Duncan* – digital

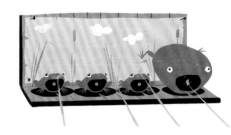

(BELOW) *Candy Apple interior concept* • *Griselda Sastrawinata* – digital   (ABOVE & RIGHT) *Game concepts* • *Jon Klassen* – digital

(Right) **Ride concept** • *Peter Maynez* – digital
(Far Right) **Game design** • *Paul Westacott* – digital

Far Far Away

FAR FAR AWAY is the kind of idyllic place that one dreams of raising a family in. Good schools, happy citizens, and a thriving local economy keep the magical kingdom at peace. Even the fairytale creatures have found their own ways to contribute to this utopian settlement. The Muffin Man, Gingy, and the Big Bad Wolf all now work at the Candy Apple, and Pinocchio has taken up a very respectable profession as a bookseller at Canterbury Books.

To assist the visual development team, producer Gina Shay got out her measuring spoons and started to bake. "I made the cake for two reasons,"
explains Shay. "Art reference and, second and more importantly, story proof of concept. I wanted to make a cake so obnoxious in appearance that anyone could understand why Shrek would smash it."

(ABOVE) ***Birthday cake*** · *Gina Shay, with help from Miles (5) and Nina (3) Bakshi* – mixed ingredients
(LEFT) ***Shrek picks up the cake*** · *Griselda Sastrawinata* – digital

29

(BELOW) **Boookstore sign** • *Leighton Hickman* – digital
(RIGHT) **Canterbury Books bookstore** • *Paul Westacott* – digital
(BOTTOM) **Rumpelstiltskin at the bookstore** •
Tianyi Han – digital

(BELOW) *Three Pigs' houses* • *Paul Westacott* – marker

(ABOVE) *Gingy's babes costume designs* • *Natalie Franscioni-Karp* – digital
(BELOW) *Far Far Away flyover concept* • *Natalie Franscioni-Karp* – digital

The Visit

PARENTS WILL DO ANYTHING to protect their children, even if that means making a deal with the devil. Or, in the case of King Harold and Queen Lilian, making a deal with Rumpelstiltskin. Flash back to the first Shrek film, when Princess Fiona's curse has yet to be lifted, she is living in a dragon-guarded tower, and her parents are still at a loss as to what to do about their daughter's tragic fate. On a recommendation from King Midas, the king and queen cross class borders and venture into Far Far Away's underworld to consult with Rumpelstiltskin. Rumpel confirms he can free Fiona from her curse. In exchange, King Harold must give the Kingdom of Far Far Away to Rumpel. But just as Harold is about to sign away his kingdom, a royal messenger bursts through the door with the news that the princess has been saved! Rumpelstiltskin's plan to gain control of the kingdom is thwarted and Rumpel vows to get revenge on the ogre who spoiled his plans: Shrek.

(RIGHT) **Royal carriage** • *Paul Duncan* – digital
(BELOW) **Carriage park road lighting key** • *Leighton Hickman* – digital

(BELOW) *Witch carriage concept sketches* • *Jon Klassen* – digital
(BOTTOM) *Carriage park entrance lighting key* • *Leighton Hickman* – digital

Crone's Nest Carriage Park

BLEAK, DISMAL, AND GREY, Crone's Nest Carriage Park contrasts rather starkly with the bright and cheery streets of Far Far Away. The production team designed the carriage park to resemble an RV campground, where witches of all ages, shapes, and sizes have parked themselves and ply their trade. "We basically asked ourselves, 'Where would Rumpel live?'" explains Mitchell. "Since Rumpel is the kind of villain who wants to be surrounded by other villains, placing him in a carriage park full of fairytales' most evil characters was a natural."

Despite the rundown appearance of the carriage park and the trailers that occupy it, Rumpel has managed to carve out a respectable business for himself. Both the exterior and interior of his personal abode are modest, but reflect his personal style. Although his carriage is a far cry from the ostentatious palace to come, the filmmakers made a point of designing distinctly "Rumpel" elements in both. "We wanted certain architectural elements, such as the use of gothic arches, to remain consistent," says Zaslav.

Details in Rumpel's carriage, such as the trademark "R" painted on the central cabinet and on the mirror, foreshadow the ubiquitous "R" monograms found throughout the palace. The dominant teal, orange, gold, and scarlet colors of the curtains, wardrobe, and props are carried through into the alternate reality of Rumpel's palace. "And the centerpiece chandelier in the carriage morphs into the over-the-top disco ball in the palace," adds Zaslav.

(ABOVE) ***Witch carriage concept*** • *Peter Maynez* – digital
(BELOW) ***Witch carriage sketches*** • *Walt Dohrn* – digital

(RIGHT) ***Carriage park sign*** • *Paul Duncan* – digital
(OPPOSITE TOP) ***Carriage park concept*** • *Felix Yoon* – digital
(OPPOSITE BOTTOM) ***Carriage park entrance*** • *Leighton Hickman* – digital

PART 2

A Day for a Day

Rumpelstiltskin

WITH SUCH ESTABLISHED VILLAINS as Lord Farquaad, Prince Charming, and Fairy Godmother, all of whom were extremely memorable foils to Shrek and Fiona, the production team had its work cut out for it when it set out to create an antagonist intent on ruining Shrek and Fiona's happiness in *Shrek Forever After*. "The villains from all the Shrek films are so great," says head of story Walt Dohrn. "We asked ourselves, 'What do we do to get to that level of villain?'"

Naturally, the story team turned to fairytales for inspiration, cracking open the classic compendium by the Brothers Grimm from 1812. Among the most memorable was the story of Rumpelstiltskin, a dwarf who visits a miller's daughter who has been locked away in a tower and ordered by her king to spin straw into gold or face execution. Rumpel, of course, can perform the impossible task, and asks for the daughter's firstborn in exchange for stepping in. A cautionary tale about the consequences of making promises and deals, the story of Rumpelstiltskin opened up lots of possibilities when linked to the green ogre at the center of DreamWorks Animation's fractured fairytale world.

"We pretty much knew from the outset that Rumpelstiltskin would be our villain," says executive producer Aron Warner. "We just didn't know what kind of villain he'd turn out to be." What the crew also did not know was just how prominent a role Rumpel would eventually play in the film. Originally, they thought there would be more than one villain, but as development progressed, Rumpel's strong personality began to take shape and he came to the foreground as Shrek and Fiona's primary antagonist.

In developing the look and style of Rumpel, the filmmakers wanted to get as far away as possible from the previous villains. "Fairy Godmother and Charming are very eloquent characters," says Dohrn. "We went to the opposite end of that spectrum and went for a character who was ratty and scummy, but charming at the same time."

Director Mike Mitchell summarizes his thinking regarding Rumpel's character with a strong and simple image: "You know the guy who wins the $200 million mega lottery jackpot and doesn't *really* know how to spend the money? That's Rumpel."

That was more than enough direction for character designer Patrick Mate, who set out to visualize what a heightened version of the classic fairytale character would look like in the Shrek universe. "In the beginning, he was modeled a little bit after one of those salesmen who'd sell you a watch on the street," says Mate. "Then our designs morphed a bit and we went towards more of a ratlike face and tail."

Eventually, the character design team settled on a look that was more grounded in human anatomy—Boas's, in fact. "Max Boas, Mike Hernandez, and I sat with head of modeling Josh West to perfect the sculpting of Rumpel's face in Maya, zooming in on certain details, getting really specific," recalls production designer Peter Zaslav. "When we got to the chin, we had Max turn his head to reference his profile. That look really stuck. Rumpel has Max's chin."

(PREVIOUS) *Rumpelstiltskin's palace concept* • *Mike Hernandez* – digital
(ABOVE) *Rumpelstiltskin concept* • *J. J. Villard* – mixed media

(ABOVE) *Rumpelstiltskin's hand with quill* • *Max Boas* – digital
(OPPOSITE) *Rumpelstiltskin concept* • *Griselda Sastrawinata* – digital

A

B

C

D

E

H

I

J

K

Rumpelstiltskin sketches • *Patrick Mate* – A & F: pencil, *Mike Mitchell* – B: marker, H: pencil,
Max Boas – C, G, K, M & N: pencil, *Mike Hernandez* – D: pencil & digital, E & L: pen & ink, I & J: pencil

(OPPOSITE LEFT) *Poor Rumpelstiltskin concept* • *Mike Hernandez* – digital
(OPPOSITE RIGHT) *Rumpelstiltskin's party outfit concept* • *Mike Hernandez* – digital

Soon after, Mate was shown the caricature of Boas. "We all ended up laughing and loving it,'" recounts Mate. "We picked it because the caricature was just perfect for the design we were looking for."

As Rumpel's look was being fleshed out, so was the story. It fell to Dohrn, as head of story, to occasionally read as Rumpel opposite the voice talent during their recording sessions. Dohrn, with Mitchell directing, started to play around with vocal inflections and styles. These spontaneous performances were incorporated into story reels, bringing the character to life in the eyes and ears of the crew. Eventually, Dohrn was formally cast as Rumpel. "Walt's performance really sealed the deal on this character," says Jason Reisig, head of character animation. "When we heard him doing the temporary Rumpel test voice in our story reels, we just fell in love with the character."

Dohrn continued to play with various inflections for Rumpel's voice, even outside the recording studio. For inspiration, he looked to many striking performances, among them Sean Penn's portrayal of Daulton Lee in *The Falcon and the Snowman*. "We liked [Penn's] energy and the feeling that he was just about ready to blow up at any second, while at the same time being funny, rhythmical, and fast in his delivery," notes Dohrn. On the opposite end of the influence spectrum he cites Bette Davis's classic performance in *What Ever Happened to Baby Jane?* (deadpans Dohrn: "Drama.")

Dohrn's favorite Rumpel lines from the film are not really lines at all, but rather sounds and noises made during the course of the recording sessions—what filmmakers refer to as "efforts." "What I like the most is when he sounds like either a monkey or a goat and when he gets so excited that just tiny little voices, little sounds come out of his mouth as he goes about his business."

The end result of these collective efforts—the look, personality, and voice of Rumpel—won praise from the entire crew. "Rumpel is a wonderful villain," says visual effects supervisor Doug Cooper. "He's silly and sinister at the same time; he's ridiculously outrageous—all the things you wouldn't expect of a master villain—and that's what makes him so much fun to watch."

(ABOVE) *Rumpelstiltskin concept* • *J. J. Villard* – mixed media

Derek Drymon – digital

Maggie Kang – digital

Paul Fisher – digital

Rejean Bourdages – digital

Ryan Crego – digital

Walt Dohrn – digital

Derek Drymon – digital

Greg Miller – digital

Maggie Kang – digital

Walt Dohrn – pencil

Walt Dohrn – pencil

Paul Fisher – digital

Rejean Bourdages – digital

Ryan Crego – digital

Walt Dohrn – pencil

Maggie Kang – digital

Paul Fisher – digital

Ryan Crego – digital

Walt Dohrn – pencil

Derek Drymon – digital

Maggie Kang – digital

Ryan Crego – digital

Walt Dohrn – pencil

Maggie Kang – digital

Ryan Crego – digital

Walt Dohrn – pencil

Derek Drymon – digital

Maggie Kang – digital

Ryan Crego – digital

Walt Dohrn – pencil

Ryan Crego – digital

Walt Dohrn – pencil

Derek Drymon – digital

Walt Dohrn – pencil

Derek Drymon – digital

Walt Dohrn – pencil

Mike Mitchell – digital

Ryan Crego – digital

Walt Dohrn – pencil

Walt Dohrn – pencil

> "Rumpel's so devious and so smart that he can just put on this innocent air of trust and trick people."
> —*Gina Shay*, producer

(BELOW) *Rumpelstiltskin maquette* • *Patrick Mate* – sculpey
(RIGHT) *Rich Rumpelstiltskin concept* • *Peter Zaslav & Max Boas* – digital

(Above & Below) *Expression studies* • *Patrick Mate* – pencil
(Left) *Rich Rumpelstiltskin concept* • *Peter Zaslav & Max Boas* – digital
(Opposite Left) *Rumpelstiltskin's poor costume concept* • *Max Boas* – digital
(Opposite Right) *Rumpelstiltskin's rich costume concept* • *Max Boas* – digital

The Rumpled Look

WHEN IT COMES TO Rumpel's wardrobe choices, to say he has his own unique style would be an understatement. Although the filmmakers decided that the color palette for Rumpel's shabby clothes would be rather dull and muted (fitting his station and environment), once Far Far Away receives a radical makeover, so does he. Gone is the drab suit and in comes the garish white suit highlighted with splashes of gold and blood red. "He has all the riches, but none of the taste," says Mitchell. Part pinball-wizard-meets-Marie-Antoinette, Rumpelstiltskin dresses elaborately for every meeting, party, and occasion. Some of the most important accessories in his wardrobe are interchangeable wigs designed to suit not only the situation, but his mood and temperament as well. "There's a business wig, a victory wig, and an angry wig," says producer Gina Shay. "We used to have business shoes and party shoes," she adds, "but we decided we went just a little overboard and dialed back the boat-in-the-hair and elevator shoes. Where we pulled back to ended up being the perfect balance of accessories for Rumpel."

> "Rumpel's kind of got [art director] Max Boas's hair — a little like he just woke up."
>
> —*Walt Dohrn*, head of story and voice of Rumpelstiltskin

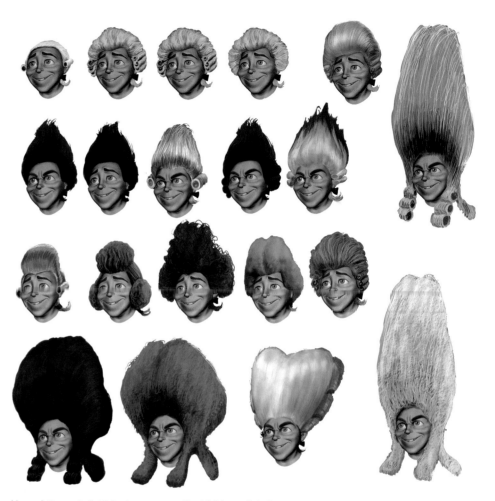

(ABOVE) *Rumpelstiltskin's wig concepts* • *Patrick Mate* – digital

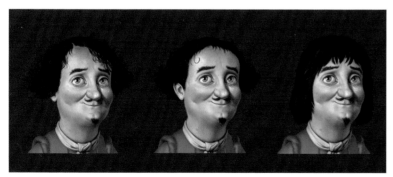

(ABOVE) *Rumpelstiltskin's hairstyle concepts* • *Mike Hernandez & Patrick Mate* – digital
(RIGHT) *Rumpelstiltskin's angry wig lighting key* • *Max Boas* – digital

(OPPOSITE TOP) *Rumpelstiltskin's victory wig* • *Leighton Hickman & Peter Zaslav* – digital
(OPPOSITE BOTTOM) *Rumpelstiltskin concept* • *Guillaume Aretos* – digital
(OPPOSITE FAR RIGHT) *Rumpelstiltskin's party outfit* • *Mike Hernandez* – digital

(ABOVE) *Rumpelstiltskin's witches concept* • *J. J. Villard* – mixed media

(Above) *Palace dining room* • *Tianyi Han & Felix Yoon* – digital

Fifi

BEFORE SETTLING on the classic fairytale character of a goose to be Rumpel's pet and sidekick, the filmmakers considered a few other possibilities. Among them were a team of six tiny, colorful unicorns, an old nag with a cardboard unicorn horn, and even a giant spider, which, as Mitchell says, would have "made Rumpel way too evil."

Ultimately, the team decided to stick with an animal that "felt" like Rumpel. Initially just an average goose that provides quills for Rumpel's contract signings, Fifi evolves into more than a pet by the time we see her again in the alternate reality. Now living a charmed life, her every need is tended to by Rumpel (who considers himself her daddy), although the Three Little Pigs are the ones who take care of Fifi on a daily basis.

(Above) *Fifi concept sketch* •
Mike Mitchell – mixed media
(Left) *Fifi character design* • *Patrick Mate* – digital
(Below) *Fifi portrait* • *Leighton Hickman* – digital

(Below) *Rumpelstiltskin's VIP screen* • *Max Boas* – digital

"By design, Fifi serves as a subtle reminder of the passage of time, appearing much larger and presumably older in the alternate reality."

—*Mike Mitchell*, director

Witches

To run his mighty empire, Rumpelstiltskin employs an army of witches, all of whom have their humble beginnings in the Crone's Nest Carriage Park. "When Rumpel strikes it rich, he takes all his friends with him, kind of like what Eddie Murphy's character does with his buddies in *Trading Places*," says Mitchell.

Early concepts show the various directions the production took in developing a distinct look for the final two types of witches. The military unit, whose primary task is to hunt ogres, serves as Rumpel's law enforcement agency, complete with armor and magical weaponry. For the "party witches," initial ideas for their look drew on '60s go-go outfits and fantasy French maid ensembles. Their final design mixed these more contemporary inspirations with classic medieval details to blend in with the festive atmosphere of the palace's ballroom.

"It's hard to do a short skirt and stay true to the medieval times."
—*Mike Mitchell*, director

(Top) ***Palace party witch concepts*** • *Griselda Sastrawinata* – digital
(Above) ***Palace witch finals*** • *Mike Hernandez* – digital
(Left) ***Guard witch concept*** • *Griselda Sastrawinata* – digital
(Right) ***Guard witch final*** • *Patrick Mate* – digital
(Opposite) ***Palace witches concept*** • *Griselda Sastrawinata* – digital

Rumpel's Carriage

RUMPELSTILTSKIN'S EGG-SHAPED CARRIAGE, shown below in the run-down Crone's Nest Carriage Park, serves as a visual reference throughout the film. The oval form of his first humble abode provides the basis for a running motif used throughout his remodeled palace in the second half of the story. As Zaslav succinctly explains, "Rumpel transforms the castle of Far Far Away into a giant replica of his egg-shaped carriage."

(OPPOSITE TOP LEFT) *Carriage concept* • *Jon Klassen* – digital
(OPPOSITE MIDDLE LEFT) *Carriage concept* • *Griselda Sastrawinata* – digital
(OPPOSITE BOTTOM LEFT) *Shrek meets Rumpelstiltskin* • *Mike Hernandez* – digital
(OPPOSITE RIGHT) *Carriage color concepts* • *Jon Klassen* – digital

(ABOVE) *Carriage concept* • *Felix Yoon & Max Boas* – digital

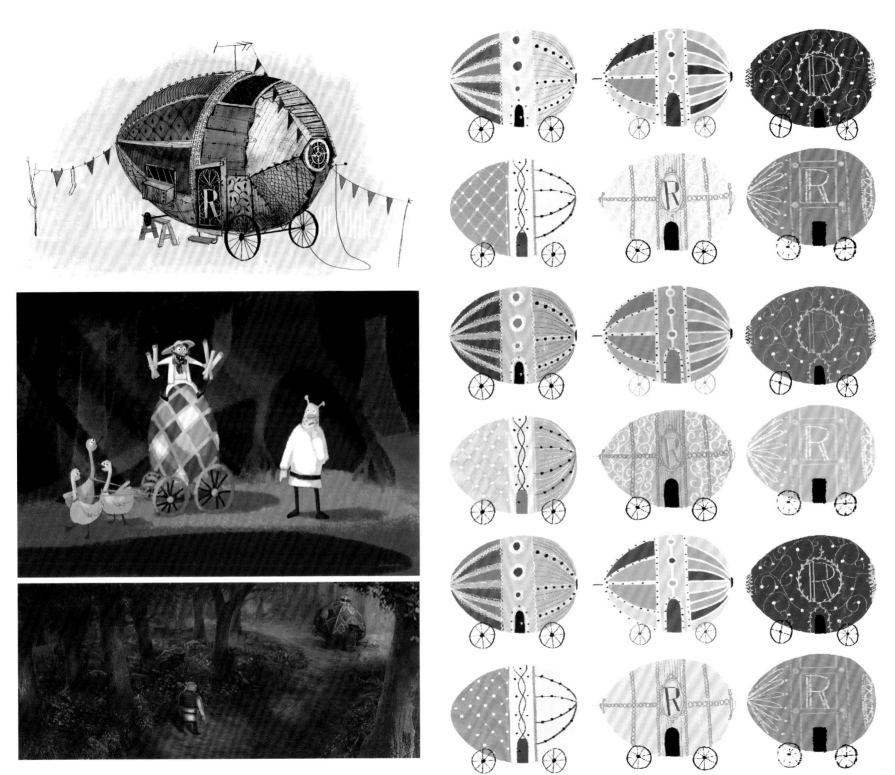

(LEFT) *Carriage interior concept* •
Peter Maynez – digital

(Below) **Rumpelstiltskin's deal concept** • *Peter Zaslav & Max Boas* – digital

(Above Left) **Carriage set pieces** • *Peter Maynez* – digital
(Above Right) **Assorted office props** • *Felix Yoon & Peter Maynez* – digital

The Contract

WHEN RUMPEL presents the contract that will exchange a day of Shrek's life for a day of unfettered ogre play, all Shrek sees is a complicated legal document made even more complex by its baroque fairytale style. "The contract is sort of the embodiment of Rumpel on paper," explains Zaslav. "Griselda Sastrawinata developed the look of the contract, which underwent many changes as both the story and the character of Rumpel evolved."

It is later revealed by Donkey (thanks to his "polygonic foldability skills") that yet another layer of complexity is hidden within the document—once it is folded correctly, an "exit clause" appears: "True Love's Kiss" will free Shrek from his alternate reality and allow him to reclaim everything he lost when he signed on Rumpel's dotted line.

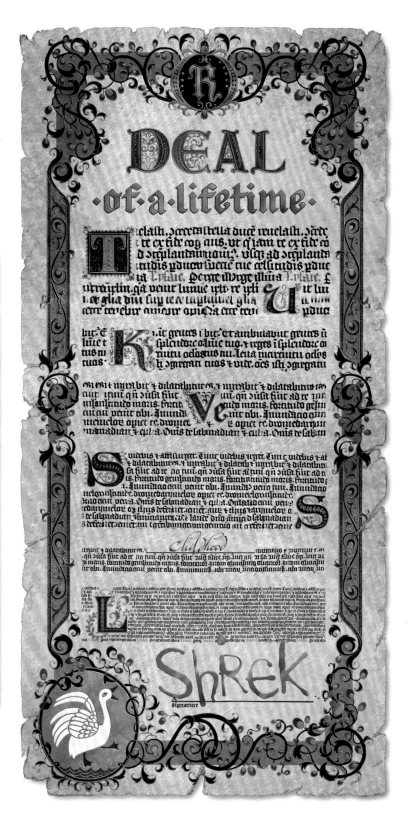

(ABOVE LEFT) *Rumpelstiltskin's quill* • *Leighton Hickman* – digital
(ABOVE) *Rumpelstiltskin's ink bottle & desk drawer* • *Felix Yoon* – digital
(ABOVE RIGHT) *Real Boy for Life contract design* • *Griselda Sastrawinata* – digital
(RIGHT) *Deal of a Lifetime contract design* • *Griselda Sastrawinata* – digital

(Above & Right) *True Love's Kiss exit clause* •
Griselda Sastrawinata – digital

61

Transforming Shrek's Reality

THE MOMENT HE SIGNS the deal with Rumpel, Shrek's world is torn to shreds as he is thrown into an alternate world that at first appears to be a mirror image of the one he's left behind. But that familiarity soon gives way as he begins to discover that he is no longer in the Far Far Away he knows.

The final realization comes when Shrek is attacked by Rumpel's henchwomen, the witches, in his empty swamp. Armed with pumpkin smoke bombs, they capture Shrek and cart him off to a face-to-face meeting with Rumpel. Fortunately, Shrek sees a ray of hope when he realizes that Donkey is pulling the wagon he's caged in. Donkey, however, looks worse for the wear and is sorely in need of a day at the groomer.

While the inherent risk of remaking Shrek's world and placing the characters in an entirely new situations was on the minds of the entire of crew, executive producer Aron Warner knew that the strong personality

of each character would accommodate this dramatic change of scenery. "The real secret is to ground stuff in the reality we already know," he explains. "Deep down, they are the same characters that audiences know and love, so long as they behave and act the same way they would under normal circumstances."

To illustrate his point, Warner refers to the scene where Shrek and Donkey first meet in the alternate reality. Shrek has finally figured out what has happened and is at his lowest. "He reconnects with Donkey and, despite the alternate world, you see that the core of the relationship is the same."

Responding to new environments or circumstances is one thing, but when it came to shifting the looks of Donkey and Puss In Boots, the production crew had to re-engineer its approach to animation, rigging, and modeling. Animators had to keep Donkey's enthusiasm bubbling to the surface, even though he's under the lash of the witches. And they

(Opposite) *Transition to alternate reality concept* • *Peter Zaslav* – digital
(Right) *Donkey's paddy wagon* • *Peter Maynez* – digital
(Below) *Witches capture Shrek* • *Paul Duncan* – digital

"At his core, he's basically the same Donkey we all know and love."
—*Patrick Mate*, character designer

had to preserve Puss's cleverness and sly delivery while he's living the life of a spoiled, overweight house cat. "It's a delicate line because you want to be true to the character's personality," explains Reisig.

Developing new looks for Donkey and Puss was also daunting. Puss's increased volume implied significant changes to the modeling and rigging of the feline. The revisions to Donkey's look were primarily due to his ill-groomed pelt. "Since the fur is longer, we had to make sure the skin of the model didn't intersect itself," explains Oliver Finkelde, head of character effects.

Although they are basically the same characters they were in the previous films, the altered designs for each character brought a freshness to the whole process. "It feels like you're animating them for the first time, even though we all know them," says supervising animator Marek Kochkout.

Donkey Without an Ogre

IN THE ALTERNATE REALITY OF Far Far Away, Donkey is still the same lovable character audiences know well, with the same winning personality and sense of humor. He's just fallen on hard times and is now in the employ of Rumpel's witches, pulling their paddy wagon on their missions to find and capture ogres. "He's lost his clean-shaven look and now looks like he's been homeless for about a hundred years," says Mate. "In our initial design [below], we went way further than what actually made it into the movie."

"Donkey never fails to make me laugh. Eddie Murphy's performance is so amazing and there is so much energy in this new dynamic between him and Shrek."
—*Walt Dohrn*, head of story and voice of Rumpel

(ABOVE) *Alternate reality Donkey* • *Patrick Mate* – digital
(OPPOSITE TOP LEFT) *Donkey & witches on the way to Far Far Away* • *Max Boas* – digital
(OPPOSITE TOP RIGHT) *Wagon cage model* • *Peter Maynez* – digital
(OPPOSITE BOTTOM) *Alternate reality look development* • *Mike Hernandez* – pencil

Puss (Out Of Boots)

NO LONGER THE RACONTEUR first encountered in *Shrek 2*, Puss In Boots has traded his classic footwear for a pretty new bow and now lives the life of a spoiled house cat, complete with a kitty condo and all the cream he can drink. Drastically altering the dashing design of such a favorite character made more than a few people a little jittery. "We had to take advantage of the alternate reality," says Mitchell. "Although we all loved the alternate Puss design from the beginning, it wasn't fully embraced until we saw the final image of him sliding down his scratching post. The alternate Puss is now one of everyone's favorite parts."

(ABOVE) *Milk bar* • *Leighton Hickman* – digital
(LEFT) *Puss's comb & brush* • *Leighton Hickman* – digital
(BELOW) *Puss's cat condo* • *Leighton Hickman* – digital
(FAR LEFT & OPPOSITE) *Alternate reality Puss concepts* • *Patrick Mate* – digital

"Puss is a little bit fluffier, so we had to deal with a lot of interpenetrations on the skin, which then makes it harder to simulate the fur."

—*Oliver Finkelde,*
head of character effects

Fairytale Characters' New Vocations

WORKING WITHIN THE ALTERNATE REALITY framework, the story team was able to turn the world of the fairytale characters completely upside down. With the exception of Gingy, who's a gingerbread gladiator, the fairytale characters all now work for Rumpel. Once the biggest and baddest wolf in all of Far Far Away, Wolfie is now Rumpel's personal wig valet; Pinnochio begs for just one good deal; and the Three Little Pigs tend to Rumpel's pet goose, Fifi.

(ABOVE) *Storyboard sequence* • *Joel Crawford* – digital

(ABOVE) *Storyboard sequence* • *Maggie Kang* – digital   (BELOW) *Gingy fight* • *Felix Yoon* – digital

(ABOVE) *Pinnochio concept* • *Griselda Sastrawinata* – digital

(ABOVE) *Alternate reality Wolfie in disguise turnaround* •
Natalie Franscioni-Karp – digital
(BELOW) *Alternate reality Little Pig turnaround* •
Paul Duncan – digital
(RIGHT) *Fairytale characters* • *Paul Duncan* – digital

(ABOVE) *Alternate Gingy fight storyboards* • *Bryan Andrews* – digital

 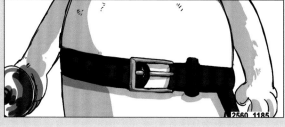 

(ABOVE) *Alternate Puss In Boots storyboards* • *Joel Crawford* – digital

(ABOVE) *Alternate Three Little Pigs storyboards* • *Derek Drymon, Paul Fisher & Ryan Crego* – digital

Early storyboard explorations show the fairytale characters in their new alternate reality lives: Gingy battling animal crackers in a makeshift gladiatorial arena; Puss reclaiming his boots; the Three Little Pigs as Rumpel's servants; and Donkey being eaten by Dragon. "Mike Mitchell's boards are very simple and illustrative," says Shay. "He stages everything with comedy and character in mind. When his 'Dragon eats Donkey' scene went into 3D layout and was restaged with more sophisticated camera angles and added depth, it just wasn't as funny anymore. We ended up having to mimic Mike's boards almost exactly to preserve and highlight the comedy of the scene."

(ABOVE) *Alternate Donkey ending storyboards* • *Mike Mitchell* – digital

Shrek's Perfect Day

AS IF TAKING A STROLL DOWN MEMORY LANE, Shrek enjoys the good old days when seeing an ogre incited a scream of terror, rather than a shriek of excitement from a sightseeing tourist. Terrorizing farmers, disrupting a wedding, and generally wreaking havoc in town is exactly the perfect day he had in mind when he signed Rumpel's contract.

(RIGHT) *Village pig trough concept sketch* • *Ron Kurniawan* – pen & ink

(ABOVE) *Village building concepts* • *Max Boas* – pen & ink
(BELOW) *Village building designs* • Design – *Paul Westacott*, Color – *Natalie Franscioni-Karp* – digital

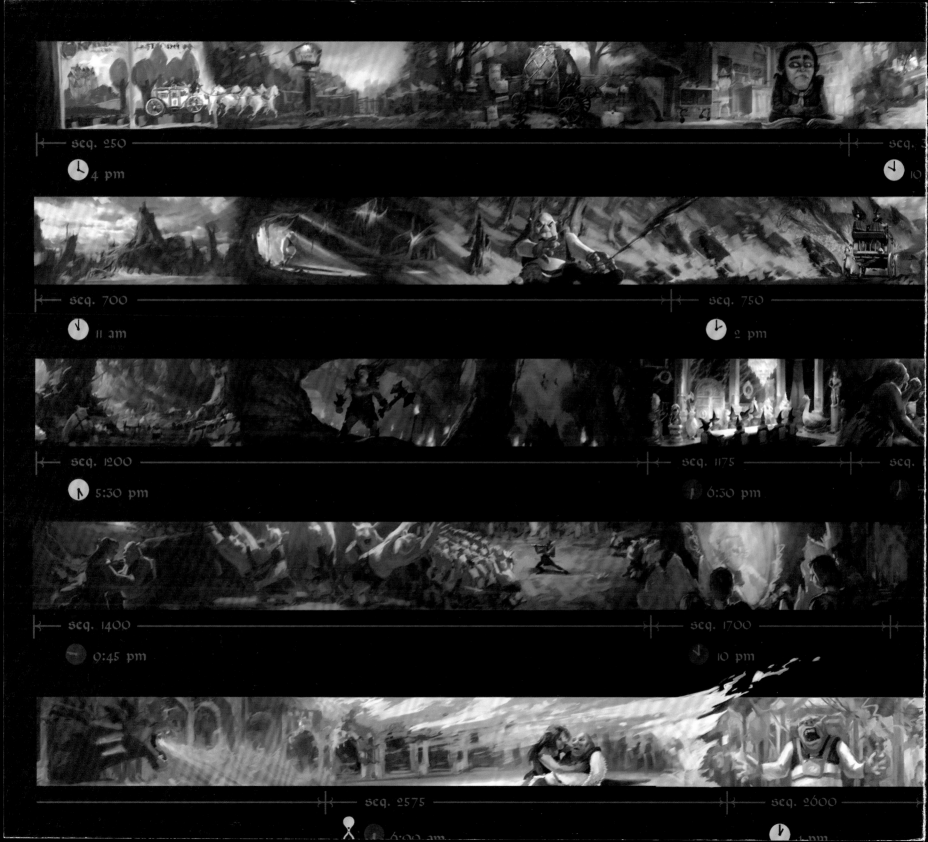

seq. 250

4 pm

seq. 3

10

seq. 700

11 am

seq. 750

2 pm

seq. 1200

5:30 pm

seq. 1175

6:30 pm

seq.

seq. 1400

9:45 pm

seq. 1700

10 pm

seq. 2575

6:00 am

seq. 2600

pm

(Below) **Hand puppet designs** • *Ron Kurniawan* – digital
(Bottom) **Shrek's perfect day** • *Paul Duncan* – digital

The Color Script

A REPRESENTATION of the visual tenor of every scene in the film laid out according to a timeline, the color script for *Shrek Forever After* was a collaboration between Zaslav, Hernandez, Boas and their teams. The color script for the film serves as a way for the filmmakers to see how the characters interact with the environment and, in a subtle way, provides an emotional roadmap for the film.

Initially, the color and look of *Shrek Forever After* is reminiscent of the three previous Shrek films, albeit a little brighter and more colorful. Once Shrek signs

seq. 650

6:00 – 9:00 am

seq. 1125

4:30 pm

seq. 1250

8:45 pm

seq. 1775

9:30 pm

seq. 2550

5:15 am

seq. 2560

5:30 am

(Gatefold) *Shrek's perfect day* • *Max Boas* – digital
(Above) *Color script* • *Mike Hernandez & Max Boas* – digital

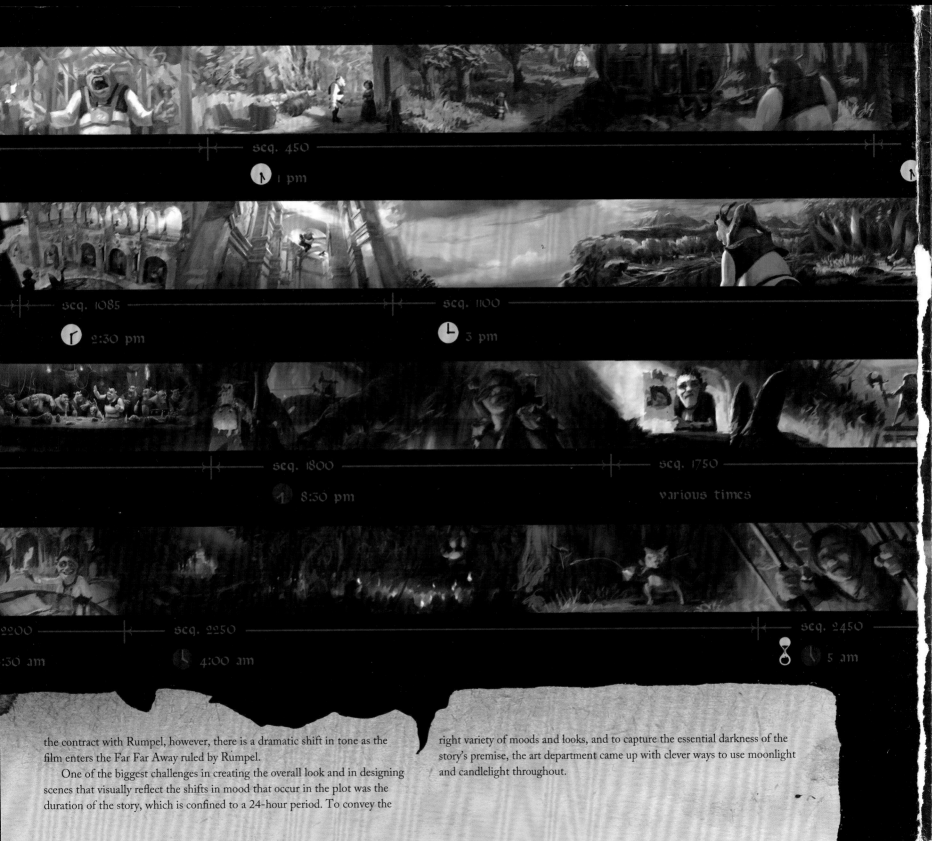

seq. 450

1 pm

seq. 1085

2:30 pm

seq. 1100

3 pm

seq. 1800

8:30 pm

seq. 1750

various times

seq. 2200

seq. 2250

4:00 am

seq. 2450

5 am

the contract with Rumpel, however, there is a dramatic shift in tone as the film enters the Far Far Away ruled by Rumpel.

One of the biggest challenges in creating the overall look and in designing scenes that visually reflect the shifts in mood that occur in the plot was the duration of the story, which is confined to a 24-hour period. To convey the

right variety of moods and looks, and to capture the essential darkness of the story's premise, the art department came up with clever ways to use moonlight and candlelight throughout.

Captured at the Swamp House

AFTER SPENDING A SEEMINGLY PERFECT DAY as the ogre he remembers from his bachelor days, Shrek returns to the ruin of the swamp house that is a far cry from the home he shares with Fiona and their ogre babies. In this scene, the filmmakers wanted the contrast between the real world and the alternate reality to be as striking as possible, to show with a single, powerful image what Shrek has lost. "This is when reality sets in for Shrek," explains producer Teresa Cheng. "He now realizes what he's lost by signing a deal with Rumpel."

(BELOW) *Shrek in the postered forest* • *Max Boas* – digital

(BOTTOM LEFT) *Shrek runs home* • *Paul Duncan* – digital

(BOTTOM MIDDLE) *Swamp witch attack* • *Paul Duncan* – digital

(BOTTOM RIGHT) *Swamp lighting key* • *Mike Hernandez* – digital

(RIGHT) *Swamp tree sketches* • *Mike Hernandez* – pencil

(OPPOSITE TOP LEFT) *Alternate swamp concept* • *Nathan Fowkes* – digital

(OPPOSITE TOP RIGHT) *Alternate swamp concept* • *Facundo Rabaudi* – digital

(OPPOSITE BOTTOM) *Alternate swamp concept* • *Peter Zaslav* – digital

Dragon's Keep—Even More Bleak

(BELOW) *Dragon's Keep stairs* • *Peter Zaslav* – digital
(OPPOSITE) *Dragon's Keep exterior* •
Natalie Franscioni-Karp – digital

WHEN SHREK REACHES the interior of Dragon's Keep, he hopes to meet Princess Fiona waiting patiently for True Love's Kiss. Instead, he finds an even more barren and desolate space than the abandoned castle he visited in the first movie. As a visual counterpoint to the bleak exterior of Dragon's Keep, filmmakers used a host of clouds to both brighten the environment and evoke a dreamlike mood that reflects Shrek's state of mind when he's confronted with the fact that things are not as they should be.

(BELOW) *Dragon's Keep interior* • *Griselda Sastrawinata* – digital   (BOTTOM) *Fiona's bedroom* • *Griselda Sastrawinata* – digital

Even Farther Away

RUMPEL'S RULE OF Far Far Away has had a significant impact on its once bright and cheery boulevards. Clearly, almost every tax dollar has been spent on the renovation of his palace and the maintenance and decoration of its impressive oval dome, leaving the downtown in shambles. Throughout the design process and the creative explorations of the various ways in which Rumpel might alter King Harold and Queen Lilian's kingdom, the giant oval dome perched high atop the castle remained the great constant—the fitting symbol of a new era of tackiness.

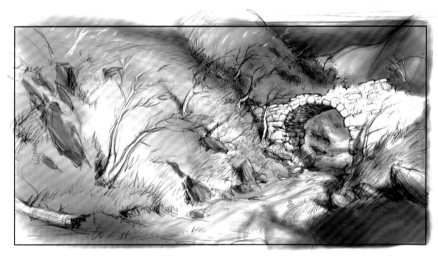

(TOP) ***Path to Far Far Away concept sketch*** • *Peter Zaslav* – digital
(ABOVE) ***Donkey on the way to alternate Far Far Away*** • *Max Boas* – digital
(RIGHT) ***Alternate Far Far Away*** • *Paul Duncan* – digital

"Mike Mitchell's initial inspiration for the design of the palace was that everything associated with Rumpel be round. He wanted to get away from the traditional way of portraying a villain as angular."

—*Peter Zaslav*, production designer

(Top) *Far Far Away at night* • *Paul Duncan* – digital   (Above) *Palace reveal* • *Max Boas* – digital   (Opposite) *Alternate Far Far Away practical model* • *Facundo Rabaudi* – mixed media

The Look of Alternate Reality

"**E**VERYTHING HAS BEEN TURNED ON ITS EAR in the alternate reality," says Cheng. "Even the landscapes and environment." Indeed, the once lush surroundings that border Far Far Away have taken a turn for the worse, as if the climate had suddenly changed. Yet as different as the landscapes appear, audiences will feel a certain sense of familiarity, as will Shrek, heightening his sense of anxiety as he moves through an uncanny version of his home surroundings. Explains Boas, "The basic shape language from Shrek's world is present; we just used color and lighting in a different way."

The key to creating this sense of strange familiarity was the development of a color script for *Shrek Forever After* that fit within the universe of all the films but worked along its edges, providing an "alternate reality" twist. Gone are the lush, towering trees of the forest and the bright meadows teeming with flowers and foliage. Verdant green valleys and hills have turned to dry grass and barren landscapes.

Sharp angles of rocks and cliffs are accentuated by the use of dramatic lighting. Says Boas, "Everything is destroyed, even the trees, which are now just stumps."

To ensure visual diversity in the face of the 24-hour "ticking clock," the artists used the sky as a device to heighten the surroundings. Ominous clouds like the ones that foreshadow a thunderstorm provided unique options for lighting. Sunlight and moonlight struggling to break through cloud cover were used to augment the mood. The dramatic shapes of the clouds and the expressionistic colors in the sky added depth and perspective to each scene by providing striking backgrounds against which the filmmakers cast Rumpel's army of patrol witches.

(Opposite Top) *Alternate reality look development sketch* • *Mike Hernandez* – pen & ink
(Opposite Bottom & Below) *Alternate reality concept* • *Leighton Hickman* – digital
(Bottom) *Alternate reality concept* • *Mike Hernandez* – digital

(Page 90 Top) *Alternate reality concept* • *Leighton Hickman* – digital
(Page 90 Bottom) *Alternate reality concept* • *Tianyi Han* – digital
(Page 91 Top) *Alternate reality concept* • *Max Boas* – digital
(Page 91 Bottom) *Alternate reality concept* • *Mike Hernandez* – digital

"Every movie we do brings a new standard. We've raised the bar in lighting, delivering images far and above what we could have hoped for."
—*Doug Cooper*, visual effects supervisor

Rumpel's Palace

IN MANY RESPECTS, it might be a blessing that King Harold and Queen Lilian are not around to witness Rumpel's garish transformation of their beloved castle and home. An extreme makeover gone horribly awry, Rumpel has taken "bad taste" to a whole new level. "This was one of our most elaborate sets on the film," says Zaslav.

Basing their dramatic redecoration of the palace on the original models of the king and queen's castle, Zaslav and Boas elaborated on the oval shape motif that was introduced with Rumpel's carriage, using it as a touchstone for the redesign of the exterior and interiors. The pointed spires gave way to a giant rounded cupola, and the square shapes were softened with rounded edges. Explains Zaslav, "We wanted to get away from the traditional way of portraying a villain as very angular and everything around him being spiky and sharp. So we went in the opposite direction, making all the shapes around him round."

Inside the palace, garish golds, bright whites, bold reds, and decadent lavenders dominate the color palette. Rumpel's pet goose, Fifi, provided inspiration for the patterned décor of many of the rooms, including Rumpel's VIP lounge, which is adjacent to the disco ballroom where the witches gather to stand, pose, party, and, most of all, dance. "Rumpel has a lot of parties," says Boas. "The floor to the disco glows orange to the pulsating music. In one of the biggest surprises of the film, the floor parts and it is revealed that the orange glow is actually the fire of Dragon."

The palace also provides the location for two of the most visually challenging sequences in the film: a high-adrenaline broom chase scene in which Shrek and Donkey escape from Rumpel's witches (*see page 98*) and the final climactic battle of the film (*see page 132*).

(ABOVE) *Exterior concept sketches* • *Mike Hernandez* – pencil
(LEFT) *Palace map* • *Peter Zaslav* – pencil & digital
(OPPOSITE) *Rumpel's palace* • *Mike Hernandez* – digital

(OPPOSITE) **King Rumpelstiltskin** •
Griselda Sastrawinata – digital
(BELOW) **Throne room floor** •
Paul Duncan – digital

(LEFT) **VIP alcove designs** •
Design - *Paul Westacott*
Color - *Felix Yoon* – digital

(Opposite Left) *Alcove concept sketch* • *Paul Westacott* – digital
(Opposite Right) *Hourglass* • *Felix Yoon* – digital
(Below) *Rumpelstiltskin statue* • *Griselda Sastrawinata* – digital
(Right) *Disco ball* • *Paul Duncan* – digital

97

The Broom Chase—A Ride Through the Production Pipeline

THE BROOM CHASE SEQUENCE is one of the most hair-raising sequences in the film. In order to escape Rumpel's palace, Shrek, a novice to broom flying, must steer an out-of-control broom through the cavernous castle while being pursued by an army of witches who toss pumpkin bombs at him. Oh, and he's got Donkey riding shotgun.

After the sequence was storyboarded by Dohrn's team, director Mitchell turned to the character modeling, rigging, layout, and visual effects teams to bring the spine-tingling sequence to life. For head of modeling Josh West, the sequence presented a welcome challenge. "On this film, we had the opportunity to build something that was extremely elaborate architecturally," says West. "It was nice to be able to fill in all those details and build something that was really ornate and enjoyable."

With Shrek being chased by a coven of witches, the sequence then called for close collaboration between the layout/pre-visualization departments and the character animation team, headed by Yong Duk Jhun and Reisig, respectively. For this key action sequence, the 3D stereoscopic camera had to be used in the most effective way possible. "Every shot composed with the stereoscopic camera is carefully controlled by the layout artists," explains Jhun.

The sheer complexity of visual detail in the palace could have hindered the action sequence, but the visual effects team was up to the task, knowing that they needed to support the goal of a visceral, 3D chase sequence in any way they could. "This is the first time we see the Shrek world through a stereoscopic view," explains Jhun. "You can actually feel the depth, like you are actually in Far Far Away and inside the castle."

Working with Boas and Zaslav, the visual effects team used the details of the palace's layout to the scene's advantage, crafting a complicated continuity and establishing a rhythm to the sequence. The team spent hours choreographing the movements of the chase through the rich, detailed environment so that all of the twists and turns through the corridors and hallways would make sense to the viewer.

Ultimately, the filmmakers wanted audiences to feel as though they are right there with Shrek and Donkey on the broom. "The dynamic camera style of the film increased the challenge for the lighting department," says Cooper. "We needed to support a camera that could take the audience anywhere in the set. Using stereo 3D adds to the depth and complexity of the shots, but also gives our work a presence and tangibility that cannot be achieved in traditional flat filmmaking."

The finishing touches to the sequence involved further challenges. "There are numerous, complex crowd effects in this film," explains Cooper. "Combining them with all the backlighting and the smoke from various sources proved very challenging."

The result of this detailed collaboration between departments is one of the most exciting scenes in the film—and a tour-de-force of CG filmmaking. Appropriately, this scene marks the transition to the second act, in which Shrek re-meets Fiona and they challenge Rumpel's rule.

1085_1399

(ABOVE) *Storyboard* • *Anthony Zeirhut* – digital, (RIGHT) *Rough layout*,
(OPPOSITE TOP) *Animation*, (OPPOSITE BOTTOM) *Final frame*

PART 3
True Love's Kiss

Fiona, Warrior Princess

(Previous Pages) *World fades concept* • *Leighton Hickman* – digital
(Below Left) *Fiona preparing for ambush* • *Peter Zaslav* – digital
(Below) *Warrior Fiona storyboards* • *Chris Reccardi* – marker
(Opposite) *Alternate reality concept* • *Max Boas* – digital

SADOV reimagines Fiona, the princess who once dreamed of becoming Mrs. Fiona Charming, as a full-on ogress who fearlessly leads the ogre resistance, determined to overthrow Rumpel's rule and ensure freedom for all ogres. A far cry from the pampered princess introduced in the first film, the Fiona of *Shrek Forever After* has traded in her tiara for a knife and battle-ax, and her gown for a leather vest and armor. A true warrior princess, Fiona has become a force to be reckoned with and feared.

The road to becoming a fearless leader was long and winding, and full of heartbreak. After spending years waiting for True Love to find her, Fiona made peace with the fact that True Love was not her destiny. Summoning her courage, she escaped Dragon's Keep and started her life over by embracing her inner ogre. Empowered, she set about uniting solitary ogres who had been living in fear. Inspired by her newfound family, she channeled all her passion and energy into her work,

determined to overthrow Rumpel and his witches. "Fiona embraces her ogreness in this movie and hides her human form from those around her," observes Jason Reisig, head of character animation. "She's been hit very poignantly by all the issues that Rumpel has brought forth, and that in turn provides her motivation as a leader."

To physically demonstrate this transformation from princess to warrior, Reisig and his team worked diligently to add subtle changes to the way Fiona was animated while at the same time keeping true to the core of the character (some of the biggest technical challenges here were with her hair; *see page 105*). "She's always been a powerful princess and not a pushover in any way," says Reisig. "But this takes her to a whole new level where she's a warrior. She also has to be Fiona, but she has to have this kind of stature to her—and toughness. It was our task to find the right balance in her movements and expressions, giving an edge to her animation while at the same time not changing who she is."

When Shrek first meets Fiona at the ogre camp, he is clearly taken aback by her transformation. And she literally has no idea who he is. Both of them, though, sense that there is a deep connection between them. "There are some beautiful moments between Shrek and Fiona where they are trying to understand why their connection is so strong, but she doesn't know him in this alternate universe," explains producer Gina Shay. "There is a scene where they are sparring, and their chemistry reminds me of two school kids who like each other and don't know what to do about it, so they just punch each other. The animators conveyed this skillfully."

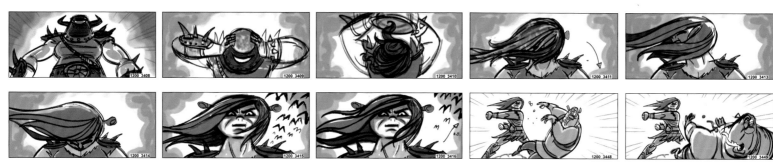

(Left & Above) *Fiona concepts* • Paul Rudish – digital

Fiona's Hair

ONE OF THE MOST NOTABLE physical changes to Princess Fiona in the alternate reality is her hairstyle. "Her hair is really a character unto itself," says director Mike Mitchell.

Animating CG hair is a complicated task, and long hair is especially difficult. "Fiona's hair is one of the most complex hairstyles we've ever animated here at DreamWorks," says visual effects supervisor Doug Cooper. "Creating such a flowing, wavy hairstyle is a huge challenge for computer graphics artists, and was very rewarding."

To tackle the troublesome strands, Cooper turned to his character effects team, lead by Oliver Finkelde. In order to achieve the desired effects, Finkelde and his team actually treated Fiona's hair like a separate character, creating an independent rigging system for the flowing red locks. The rig, however, was not without its challenges as the character effects team had to work closely with animators to ensure that both the rigs of the hair and the body would not overlap each other when either moved. "It is important to make sure those curls and waves don't intersect each other or cut into another part of the character, such as the shoulder, arm, or neck," explains Finkelde.

A few of the story moments called for Fiona to have her hair in a ponytail, creating a more manageable style. This hairstyle didn't require an independent rig and remained part of the Fiona character, simplifying the animation process. But with the technological leaps made for Fiona's long hair, and all the attention paid to the wilder mane, the final execution of her ponytail hairstyle paled in comparison. The character effects team was called in to provide tweaks to the shorter style. "Oliver's team raised the bar with the long hair they developed for Fiona," says Cooper. "It was so good, we had to go back and upgrade her ponytail for other sequences in the film to keep the quality consistent throughout."

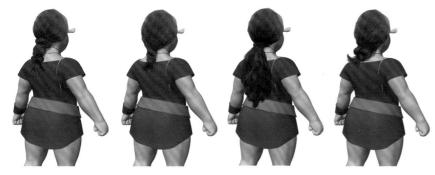

(ABOVE) **Fiona hairstyle designs** • *Patrick Mate* – digital
(RIGHT) **Fiona design** • *Walt Dohrn* – digital

(BELOW) ***Warrior Fiona final concept*** • *Patrick Mate* – digital
(OPPOSITE) ***Fiona reveal*** • *Leighton Hickman* – digital

Brogan

WHEN SHREK STUMBLES UPON A CAMPSITE populated by ogres, he realizes he's not alone in the world. There is a full-blown resistance to Rumpel's oppressive regime, made up of Shrek's ogre brethren. A warrior's life has turned them into big and strong veterans. Compared to this bunch, Shrek is the runt of the litter.

The biggest of the resistance members is Brogan, Fiona's second in command. Preliminary designs for this lieutenant tended toward the classic barbarian look, and the filmmakers named him Gnimrahc ("charming" spelled backwards). Eventually, this key commando evolved into a bigger, tougher, and smellier version of Shrek who was renamed Brogan (and voiced by a newcomer to the Shrek family, Jon Hamm).

(OPPOSITE) *Gnimrahc* • *Peter Zaslav* – digital
(LEFT) *Gnimrahc* • *Patrick Mate* – sculpey & digital
(ABOVE) *Brogan concept* • *Max Boas* – digital
(RIGHT) *Brogan concept* • *Peter Zaslav* – digital

The feet of these guys
seem too big for the ankles

(ABOVE) **Ogre concept** • *Walt Dohrn* – pen & ink
(LEFT, TOP & OPPOSITE) **Ogre concepts** • *Mike Hernandez* – pencil

Ogres

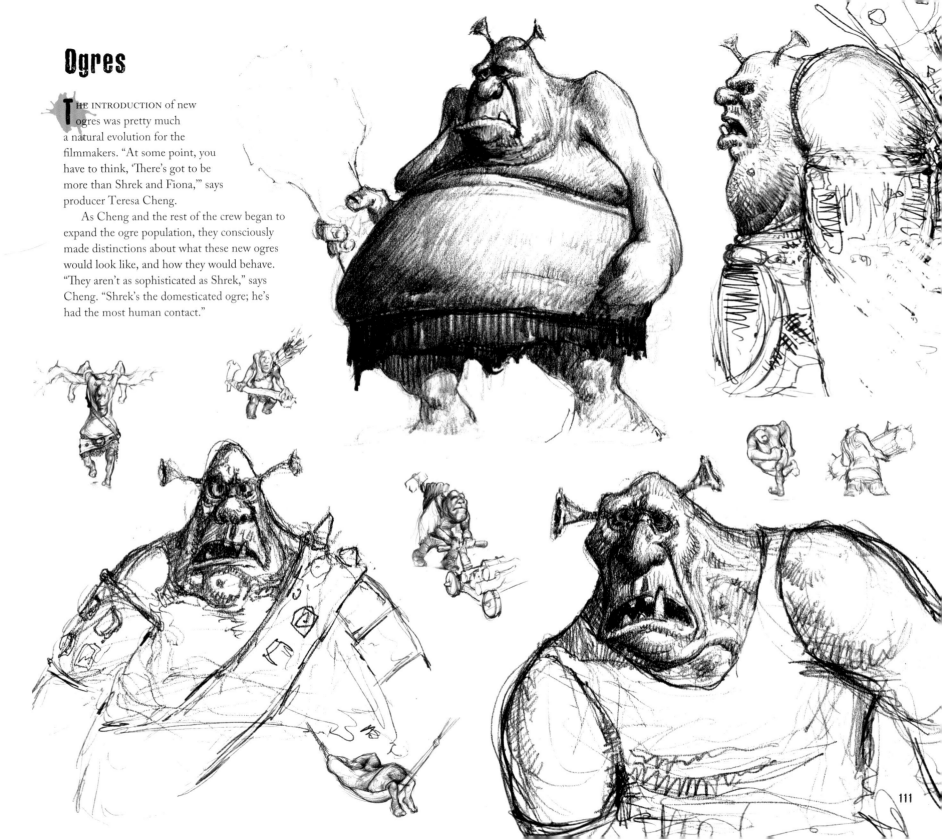

THE INTRODUCTION of new ogres was pretty much a natural evolution for the filmmakers. "At some point, you have to think, 'There's got to be more than Shrek and Fiona,'" says producer Teresa Cheng.

As Cheng and the rest of the crew began to expand the ogre population, they consciously made distinctions about what these new ogres would look like, and how they would behave. "They aren't as sophisticated as Shrek," says Cheng. "Shrek's the domesticated ogre; he's had the most human contact."

A

B

C

D

E

F

G

H

(ABOVE & BELOW) *Ogre concept lineup* • *J J Villard* – digital

I J K L M N O P Q R S

(BELOW) *Ogre concepts* • *Paul Rudish* – digital

(ABOVE & BELOW) *Ogre family portraits* • *Patrick Mate* – digital

The Ogre Camp

MODELED LOOSELY AFTER a Mobile Army Surgical Hospital, the Ogre Camp is a series of tents and hollowed-out trees that serves as a classic hideout for Fiona and her band of ogre rebels.

When developing the look of the Ogre Camp, the crew turned to the ogres and their hulking physicality for inspiration. "We designed the trees to look like big, stocky ogre legs," explains production designer Peter Zaslav. "Basically, the look of the forest is the personification of the ogres through their environment, right down to the warts on the tree trunks."

The production didn't want the camp to be a menacing, off-putting place, though, so they lit it with an inviting, hearthlike light. "We gave the Ogre Camp an overall color scheme made up of warm tones and a lot of oranges through the use of candlelight," says art director Max Boas.

(RIGHT) **Ogre Camp map** • *Peter Zaslav* – digital
(BELOW) **Ogre Camp concept** • *Griselda Sastrawinata* – digital

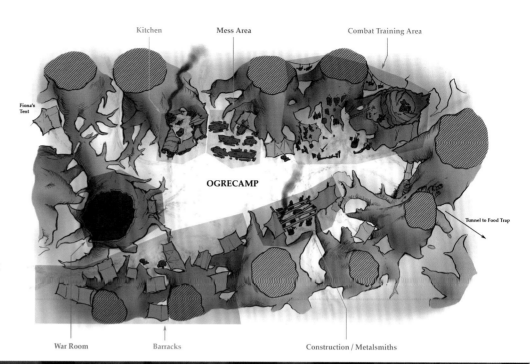

Kitchen   Mess Area   Combat Training Area

Fiona's Tent

OGRECAMP

Tunnel to Food Trap

War Room   Barracks   Construction / Metalsmiths

(Top) **Ogre swamp camouflage** • *Paul Duncan* – digital

(Left) **Ogre weapons** • *Andy Bialk* – digital

(Below) **Ogre Camp concept** • *Nathan Fowkes* – digital

(Above) **Witch dummies** • *Max Boas* – digital

(Left & Above) **Barracks and smithy** • *Leighton Hickman* – pencil

OGRE BUSH

OGRE TRUNK

(Above Left & Far Right) **Concealment ideas** • *Felix Yoon* – digital

(Above) **Ogre combat training area** • *Peter Zaslav* – digital

BUSH COVERS WEAPON STASH

(Below) **Romancing Fiona** • *Natalie Franscioni-Karp* – digital
(Right) **Ogre Camp practical model** • *Facundo Rabaudi* – mixed media
(Bottom) **Ogre Camp concept** • *Felix Yoon* – digital

Fiona's Tent

THE FIONA OF *Shrek Forever After*'s alternate reality has traded in the palace and swamp house for a bare-bones living space more befitting a renegade leader than a mother of three. The only hint of luxury: Puss's canopied kitty condo and tasseled pillow.

(ABOVE) **Gift basket & open candy box** • *Natalie Franscioni-Karp* – digital
(BELOW) **Fiona's vanity** • *Leighton Hickman* – digital
(RIGHT) **Exterior of Fiona's tent concept** • *Leighton Hickman* – digital
(OPPOSITE) **Interior of Fiona's tent concept** • *Leighton Hickman* – digial

The War Room

IN DESIGNING MANY of the key sets, the production team wanted to create intimate spaces that made the audience feel as though they were part of each scene. The ogres' War Room and its warm and detailed lighting, done with candlelight, is a great illustration of this commitment. "Our goal was to make the film an immersive, organic experience and not necessarily a CG set that is simply projected on the screen," explains Zaslav. "All the set pieces feel solid and grounded, and a lot of that is achieved through lighting design."

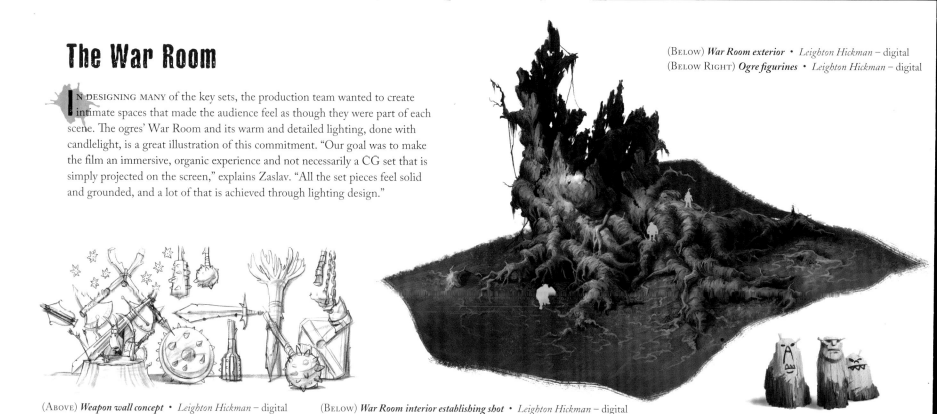

(BELOW) *War Room exterior* • *Leighton Hickman* – digital
(BELOW RIGHT) *Ogre figurines* • *Leighton Hickman* – digital

(ABOVE) *Weapon wall concept* • *Leighton Hickman* – digital   (BELOW) *War Room interior establishing shot* • *Leighton Hickman* – digital

(ABOVE) **Pine-cone carriage figurine** • *Leighton Hickman* – digital

(ABOVE) **War Room table** • *Leighton Hickman* – digital
(BELOW) **War Room interior planning** • *Leighton Hickman* – digital

The Pied Piper

NEVER UNDERESTIMATE the power of the flute. The Pied Piper, Rumpel's bounty hunter, immediately reduces the witches to helpless dancing puppets with a simple little ditty on his woodwind. "Mike Mitchell always wanted to use 'Sure Shot' by the Beastie Boys to introduce the Pied Piper," explains Cheng. "It has all the perfect elements that define how a seemingly innocuous and melodic instrument like the flute can exercise such strong control over everyone, including Rumpelstiltskin's witches."

When fashioning the look of the Pied Piper, the filmmakers took cues from the lean lines of the flute itself. The end result (opposite) is a medieval minstrel mixed with a bit of goth and a touch of British folksinger.

(RIGHT) *Pied Piper concepts* •
Andy Bialk – digital
(OPPOSITE) *Final Pied Piper concept* •
Patrick Mate – digital

(ABOVE) *Flute symbols* • *Griselda Sastrawinata* – digital

Captured!

CAUGHT BY THE hypnotic melodies of the Pied Piper's flute, the ogres fall in line (or to be more precise, a line dance). Just as Shrek and Fiona come under his spell, Donkey and Puss come to the rescue and cart them away from the enthralling sounds.

(LEFT) *Pied Piper's Fifi costume* • *Peter Maynez* – digital
(ABOVE) *Pied Piper carriage reveal concept* • *Peter Maynez* – digital
(BELOW) *Ogre march concept* • *Mike Hernandez* – digital
(OPPOSITE TOP) *Donkey & Puss to the rescue* • *Leighton Hickman* – digital
(OPPOSITE BOTTOM) *Ogres dancing* • *Leighton Hickman* – digital

Rumpel's Commercial Break

PART USED CAR SALESMAN, part devil, Rumpel devises a wicked advertising stunt to turn the citizens of Far Far Away into a massive mob intent on capturing Shrek when his roving bands of witches fail to apprehend the ogre. He uses the Magic Mirror to broadcast a slick piece of propaganda that reminds his subjects how idyllic life has become since he took over Far Far Away, and promises them the Deal of a Lifetime if they bring in the ogre who threatens their way of life.

(Right) *Pinocchio watching commercial* • *Felix Yoon* – digital
(Below) *Magic Mirror television lighting* • *Natalie Franscioni-Karp* – digital

*Hello, people, it is I, Rumpelstiltskin,
shepherd of your dreams.*

It has been my pleasure to serve you, my loyal subjects,

with top-notch service, affection, and protection.

*But recently, a certain somebody has jeopardized
our joyous lives.*

*And that somebody is the rat-munching ogre called Shrek!
That is why I come to you, dear citizens, for your help.*

*Whoever brings me this ogre shall receive . . .
the Deal of a Lifetime!*

Just think of it.

Total and complete happiness.

Dazzling, radiant fulfillment.

*All your greatest wishes. Your wildest dreams . . .
anything you could ever want. No strings attached!*

But hurry, this is a limited time offer.

*So light your torches, sharpen your pitchforks,
and get your mob on!*

(ABOVE) **Rumpelstiltskin's commercial backgrounds** • Paul Duncan – digital

The Kiss Fails

IN A KEY SCENE DURING WHICH Shrek and Fiona rediscover each other, Fiona lets down her guard just a little, telling Shrek about her lonely years locked away in the tower at Dragon's Keep. He tells her how it should have turned out—how he came to rescue her and how they found True Love. His story sounds so convincing that Fiona half believes him and, desperate after her army has been captured, kisses him, hoping that this act might save her and the ogres from Rumpel. When nothing happens, Shrek is left devastated and confused by the fact that his deal with Rumpel is still intact, as well as what this situation implies—that he and Fiona do not share True Love.

(BELOW LEFT & RIGHT) *Alternate Poison Apple design* • *Paul Westacott* – pencil & digital
(BOTTOM) *Alternate Poison Apple exterior concept* • *Tianyi Han* – digital
(OPPOSITE TOP) *The kiss fails concept* • *Peter Zaslav* – digital
(OPPOSITE BOTTOM) *Shrek rallies the troops* • *Leighton Hickman* – digital

"There's a little bit of Shrek in all of us. We're all rooting for his Happily Ever After in this final chapter."
—*Teresa Cheng,* producer

(BOTTOM) *In a sequence that was ultimately cut from the film, the Three Little Pigs, Wolfie, and Pinocchio capture Donkey and Shrek, plotting to turn him over to Rumpel in exchange for his "Deal of a Lifetime." After realizing the inherent wrongness of their actions, and seeing through Rumpel's empty promises, the fairytale characters decide to let Shrek and Donkey go.*

The Dungeon

FINALLY TOGETHER, but worlds apart, Shrek and Fiona find themselves facing certain death by Dragon in the dungeon of Rumpel's palace. This complex balancing act—both emotional and physical, via a chain and pulley system that keeps the two restrained and separated from each other—is at the heart of one of the most affecting scenes in the film. Shrek decides to let go of his selfish need to get his old life back, even if it means losing his life altogether, to help Fiona and her cause. It's then that Fiona falls for him. "In the midst of the battle, Fiona realizes that Shrek's love and feelings for her are real," says Cheng. "When Fiona looks at Shrek and says 'I've always wanted a daughter named Felicia,' we can see in her eyes that the walls around her heart are starting to crumble."

(ABOVE) ***Dungeon wall map*** • *Paul Duncan* – digital
(BOTTOM) ***Dungeon*** • *Felix Yoon* – digital

(BELOW LEFT) ***Ogres in cages*** • *Paul Duncan* – digital
(BELOW RIGHT) ***Dungeon chains*** • *Paul Duncan* – digital

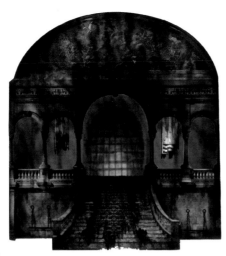

(ABOVE) **Dungeon wall map** • *Paul Duncan* – digital

(ABOVE) **Dragon & Donkey** _____ • *Felix Yoon* – digital
(BELOW) **Battle gag sketches** • *Leighton Hickman* – digital

(RIGHT) **Final battle concept** •
Felix Yoon – digital

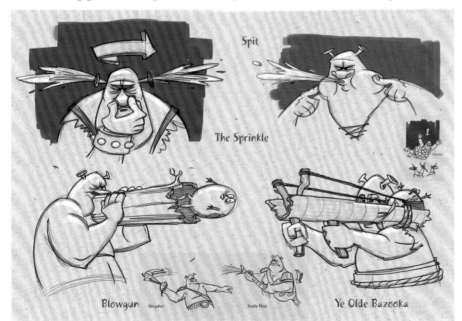

Spit

The Sprinkle

Blowgun   Slingshot   Snake Hose   Ye Olde Bazooka

The Final Battle

THE FINAL SHOWDOWN, in which the ogre army faces off against Rumpel and his witches, was a technically complex and very challenging sequence to animate. To portray hundreds of ax- and shield-wielding ogres battling a coven of witches flying through the palace, the visual effects team went into overdrive. "The scale of complexity in the Final Battle and World Fades sequences is enormous," says Alex Ongarao, head of effects.

At the centerpiece of the battle is the shiny new disco ball that Rumpel installs over the dance floor. What he doesn't realize is that it is a Trojan horse, concealing hundreds of ogres armed and ready for battle. On cue from Donkey and Puss, the silver rectangles of the disco ball start to give way, revealing the green-skinned army. This moment proved to be an enormously complicated scene to execute and required a close collaboration between the visual effects and animation teams.

The silver facets of the disco ball are actually ogre shields. When they begin to part, hundreds of characters move simultaneously. To coordinate the thousands of movements that make up this complex unfurling, and to achieve a believable look, the visual effects team orchestrated the choreography at the start of the scene, a task normally handled by the animation team. The two departments' give-and-take resulted in a breathtaking scene of visual effects and animation wizardry. "The effects team made the explosion work as if the disco ball were breaking apart, as if pushed by ogres," explains Reisig. "We then took over, creating animation cycles that we could attach to each shield, which the ogres would then follow."

(BELOW) *Chimichanga cart catapult concept* • *Max Boas* – digital
(BELOW RIGHT) *Palace escape concept* • *Mike Hernandez* – digital

(TOP) *Battle concept lighting* • *Peter Zaslav* – digital
(ABOVE) *Disco ball explodes* • *Felix Yoon* – digital

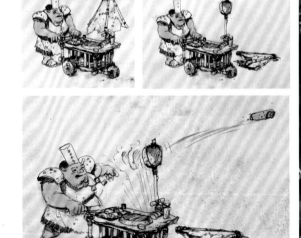

(ABOVE) **Disco ball B** • *Felix Yoon* – digital
(RIGHT) **Disco ball break sequence** •
Mike Hernandez – digital
(BELOW) **The battle** • *Peter Zaslav* – digital

World Fades

As Shrek's time runs out and he begins to fade from existence at the end of the battle, Rumpel prematurely celebrates victory while Fiona is moved to embrace the fading hero. The kiss, this time, is True Love. But is it too late? Shrek fades as the sun rises, leaving Fiona devastated. But the new dawn brings new hope. Fiona realizes that despite the sunlight, she has not reverted back to her human form. In a last-minute dramatic reversal, the alternate reality ceases to exist and begins to tear apart.

The effects in the sequence "World Fades" are both very intricate and artistically beautiful. "The world literally rips apart into shreds of paper, as if the contract were the very fabric of Rumpel's collapsing world," explains Cooper.

Shot in full stereoscopic 3D, tiny pieces of paper start to tear away from the environment, as if everything were painted on papier-mâché that has ceased to hold together. As the images are ripped away, you can actually see the torn facets of Rumpel's reality swirl around on-screen in clear stereo depth. They build into a whirlwind of thousands of flapping scraps that, fragmented, no longer add up to an environment. Rumpel's contract and storybook have been torn apart and replaced with Shrek's original world.

(Right) *Shrek fades concept* •
Paul Duncan – digital
(Opposite) *Shrek fades storyboards* •
Rejean Bourdages – digital

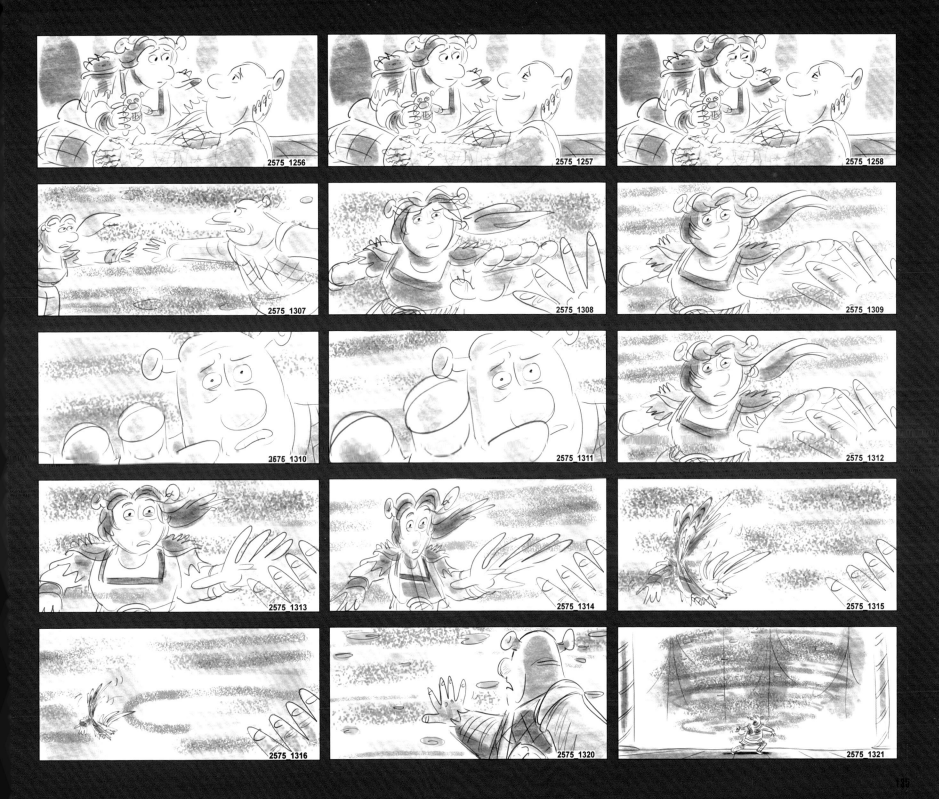

(Top) **Shrek disappears** • *Mike Hernandez* – digital
(Above) **Fiona at sunrise** • *Leighton Hickman* – digital

(Above) **Sunrise** • *Leighton Hickman* – digital
(Opposite Top) **Rumpelstiltskin's world crumbles** • *Leighton Hickman* – digital
(Opposite Bottom) **World Fades** • *Leighton Hickman* – digital

Home Again

AND IN THE BLINK OF AN EYE, Shrek is transported back to the familiar reality of the Candy Apple, surrounded by Fiona and their three children. The bright colors of the surroundings are a warm welcome home from the bleak alternate reality of Far Far Away.

(ABOVE) *Lighting color keys* • *Natalie Franscioni-Karp* – digital   (OPPOSITE) *Shrek's return concept* • *Max Boas* – digital

The Happiest Ending

SHREK FOREVER AFTER, the final chapter in Shrek's personal story, is also the end of a filmmaking journey that began in 1995 when DreamWorks Animation began the development process that would bring William Steig's fractured fairytale to the big screen for the first time. Four theatrical films, an Academy Award® for best animated feature film, two television specials (one still in the works), a Broadway musical, theme park attractions, and numerous animation and visual effects industry awards later, Shrek has become a global icon loved by millions.

For each Shrek movie it takes hundreds of people a tremendous amount of time and energy to create the images that audiences see on screen. CG animation at DreamWorks is a craft pursued by a group of passionate, talented, and dedicated artists, storytellers, and filmmakers all united by a common goal: to tell the best ogre fairytale possible. Now a true classic in its own right, the animated tale that has allowed audiences to believe in True Love in all shapes, sizes, and colors finally closes its cover. It will take its place alongside the historic fairytales that it has lovingly mocked, updated, and reinvented.

(ABOVE & OPPOSITE) *Initial end credits concepts* • *Griselda Sastrawinata* – digital
(BELOW) *Candy Apple jam band lighting key* • *Leighton Hickman* – digital

Acknowledgements

(OPPOSITE LEFT) *DreamWorks Animation crew* • Glendale, California - photo by *Mathieu Young*
(OPPOSITE INSET) *PDI/DreamWorks crew* • Redwood City, California - photo by *Luca Prasso*
(BELOW) *Ogres in action concept* • *Patrick Mate* – digital

I F I COULD MAKE A DEAL WITH RUMPEL, I'd ask that a thousand more pages be added to this book, so that we could do even more justice to the incredible work of DreamWorks Animation.

Thank you to Mike Mitchell, Teresa Cheng, Gina Shay, and Aron Warner for your time, talents, and insights on this project.

Thank you to the incredible team at DreamWorks Animation for the support and assistance that made this book possible: Belinda Arge, Tony Cosanella, Anne Globe, Michael Garcia, David Hail, Jeff Hare, Brandon Holmes, Michelle Jurado, Peter McCown, Kerry Phelan, Alissa Wright, and last but certainly not least, Kristy Cox and Carolyn Frost for making the impossible possible.

To Max Boas, Doug Cooper, Walt Dohrn, Jason Reisig, and Peter Zaslav: Thank you for your invaluable contributions. Your talents are truly inspiring! And a very special thank you to Cameron Diaz for her contribution.

I am in awe of the incredible team of publishing wizards at Insight Editions, led by Raoul Goff. Iain Morris, you're a genius. Jake Gerli, you simply rule.

And finally, thanks to those around me for being patient while I disappeared into my own alternate reality to write this book.

—*Jerry Schmitz*

Colophon

Publisher: *Raoul Goff*
Creative Director & Designer: *Iain R. Morris*
Design Assistant: *Dagmar Trojanek*
Acquiring Editor: *Jake Gerli*
Managing Editor: *Kevin Toyama*
Production Manager: *Anna Wan*

INSIGHT EDITIONS would also like to thank the talented filmmakers at DreamWorks Animation, as well as Kristy Cox, Carolyn Frost, and Corinne Combs, who made this book possible. Thank you, too, to Mark Burstein, Katherine Wright, Leslie Ann Cohen, and Binh Matthews for their work on this title.

(BELOW) **Throne room party** • *Max Boas* – digital